EMOTIONAL AND PSYCHOLOGICAL ABUSE OF CHILDREN

Kieran O'Hagan

OPEN UNIVERSITY PRESS
Buckingham

Open University Press
Celtic Court
22 Ballmoor
Buckingham
MK18 1XW

First Published 1993
Reprinted 1993, 1994, 1996

A catalogue record of this book is available from the
British Library

ISBN 0–335–09889–4 (hb.). – ISBN 0–335–09884–3 (pbk.)

Typeset by Type Study, Scarborough
Printed in Great Britain by St Edmundsbury Press Ltd
Bury St Edmunds, Suffolk

To the emotionally and psychologically abused child;
the least heard, the most easily ignored.

CONTENTS

1

COURT OUT

The Children Act (1989) stresses the importance of protecting children from all forms of significant harm. This chapter describes what happened to a fictional social worker trying to convince a court that he was protecting children from the harm of 'emotional and psychological abuse'.

Another referral! Similar allegations! Outrageous if they were true! If only these anonymous referrers could realize how difficult they made life for me. The fact that it made life hellishly difficult for the parent they were complaining about, momentarily escaped me. It was not that I suspected *their* allegations might be true; it was the expense of time and effort in proving that they were not true. These awful referrals detracted me from more serious concerns.

Jean was 24, born and reared in the city. She had a friend, or partner – I was never sure of the precise relationship – called Patrick, aged 20, born in the West Indies. Jean had two children by a former relationship with another West Indian. Her children were Mark, aged three, and Penny, aged nine months. Jean worked as a prostitute. Patrick was unemployed. Jean lived in a council house, a ghastly dilapidated cul-de-sac of about twenty houses, situated on the outer fringes of a huge sprawling post-war estate. The council may deny it, but many tenants and many social workers believed there was, if not a deliberate policy, then at least a tendency of convenience, to place mixed-race families in locations like these. Patrick lived there sometimes. Jean and her children were the only mixed-race family in the cul-de-sac. She hated it. She hated the racist abuse, the graffiti and excrement daubed on the walls; she hated the taunts directed against children too young even to understand; she hated the rumour-mongering, the gossiping circles, the conspiracies of more determined neighbours to get them removed. She hated all this, but she defied it, and, each time I imposed myself upon her to investigate yet another anonymous allegation against her, she defied it even more.

There seems to be no greater attraction to malicious and vicious referrers than a mixed-race family where the mother works as a prostitute. Nine referrals had been made about this family, alleging physical and sexual abuse, and neglect. The referrers inevitably alluded to the prostitution, irrespective of the nature of the abuse they were alleging. The allegations became increasingly explicit and outrageous: Jean was accused of conducting business in her home, in the presence of her children: 'the cars start arriving after eleven, and *it* goes on 'til the early hours'. She was accused of sharing her bed with her child Mark and her client, and she was accused of selling the use of her children for the gratification of her more perverted clients. These allegations were reinforced by additional referrals which reported that three-year-old Mark was 'teaching' all the children in the vicinity about 'things sexual'.

Neighbours glanced through half-drawn curtains as I drove slowly into the cul-de-sac. I wondered which one of them was responsible for this latest referral. None of them I'm sure were aware that I was indeed genuinely concerned about Mark and Penny. My concerns were shared by colleagues in other agencies. Both children had been admitted to hospital on a number of occasions. Mark's growth and height had repeatedly fallen below developmental milestones. The general practitioner (GP), health visitor, paediatrician and myself had all observed what we believed was an unhappy child, a withdrawn child, a child who was failing to thrive. We did not think that Penny would fare much better. We all agreed that the referrals about physical and sexual abuse were malicious – the children were periodically medically examined as a consequence of their illnesses. But we were uncertain about the reasons for the children's failure to thrive, and about that seemingly pervasive unhappiness and withdrawnness in Mark in particular. I had witnessed many disturbing scenes involving Mark and his mother. She often screamed at him for the slightest misdemeanour; she was often indifferent to his preoccupations; she often allowed him to wander for long periods throughout the cul-de-sac, and then screamed at him and smacked him if he wandered beyond it, which he invariably did. Many a time I called and found a stranger baby-sitting. Jean would be away somewhere, and not expected back that same day. Her choice of baby-sitters, obviously made in desperation, left a great deal to be desired. Any advice or stern warning on my part was met with defiance (and no shortage of verbal insults), and there was little chance of me convincing her that this was not the way to treat small children. She mocked the professionals for their stupidity and unreality. 'What do you expect me to do . . . hire a nanny!', and she always denied that her children had a problem. She claimed that she loved her children, and that she was a better mother than many around her.

As I opened the rotting, collapsing gate of their overgrown garden – no different from those on either side – I could hear yelling voices. The row between Patrick and Jean seemed more intense than usual. I slowed my pace, so that I might listen more; it seemed as though it was not merely a verbal row. I reached the door and stood there. I knocked, knowing it was futile, and that neither would reply. I asked myself what was happening to Mark and Penny; I thought the worst, and suddenly walked in, into the persistently darkened room with the thick, tattered curtains drawn across windows shut tight. What I saw frightened me as much as it angered me.

Patrick had Jean pinned to the wall with one massive hand around her throat. He was howling abuse at her. She was attempting to kick him off, and each effort provoked another punch in her ribs. She was yelling abuse back at him, but the tightening grip on her throat had the effect of hoarsening and weakening her voice. Patrick was not just pinning her to the wall, he was strangling her.

I could not see baby Penny, but I could hear her crying incessantly from beneath the hood and blankets of her ancient pram. It was a cry which I had not heard before.

Mark stood much closer. His whole countenance was gripped with terror. He was trying to scream out but his voice seemed as frozen as his feet. His mouth was wide open; his hands were clenched tight and stretched out before him. It was as if lightning or some mysterious force had stricken the child dumb, silent, terrorized and immobilized, possibly just at the very moment when he had rushed forward to try to rescue his mother, or at least to cling to her while she was being strangled. The most horrible memory was my realization that Mark knew Patrick was causing his mother's life to slowly ebb away, and that he was helpless either to stop him or to save her. Only his eyes could move and he glanced at me beseechingly. I could stop Patrick, but I could do little about the damage being done to Mark.

Some months later, I stood in the witness box of the magistrate's Family Proceedings court. During the preceding weeks, I read the file thoroughly. There were case conference minutes (three no less), medical and previous courts reports, review and financial assistance forms, assessments, countless reports of visits and hundreds of letters. The cycle of events, i.e. referrals, investigations which often made matters worse, and the occasional intervention and removal of the children, had kept repeating itself since the birth of Mark. The professionals, including myself, had distinguished themselves by getting involved at some point in responding to outrageous referrals, and on investigation became preoccupied with something else. Jean called us hypocrites when we told her that the referral had indeed turned out to be malicious but that 'we now had other concerns'. Since the last investigation, another two referrals followed: the children had been found alone one day, and Penny had twice been admitted to hospital with gastroenteritis. The nursery staff reported that Mark and mother had stopped attending, which was something of a relief to them, as they were increasingly upset by Jean's tension and rough handling of Mark when they did attend. They also reported a dramatic deterioration in Mark's hygiene. The paediatrician was alarmed, and requested a case conference. The conference shared the most up-to-date reports and assessments made by those attending, and recommended care proceedings on the grounds that the children were 'suffering significant harm' attributable to 'the care given to the children' (ss. 31(1)(a), (2)(a), (b)(i), Children Act 1989). The 'harm', for most participants, was interpreted as neglect and emotional abuse. I said I also believed the children were being 'significantly harmed' by psychological abuse. 'Same thing', someone had said, and most concurred. We all agreed that the children had not been physically or sexually abused.

In the courtroom, Mr Hastings arose to question me. He said nothing for a few moments, buttoning over his double-waisted jacket, and peering at me over his gold-rimmed, half-cut spectacles.

'Mr Morrison, if I might refer you to some extracts from your report . . . you say that the children of my client are being significantly harmed because they're being . . . "emotionally abused and neglected". Can you tell the court what that means?'

I thought for a moment, then tried to sound confident: 'it means their emotional development is being impaired'.

'What does that mean, Mr Morrison?'

His repetition of my name was obvious mockery.

'The children have emotional needs', I replied, seeing the hole he was helping me to dig for myself; 'parents have to fulfil those needs'.

'I'm not too sure the court understands you, Mr Morrison, could you expand on that?'

'I didn't think I needed to expand on it.'

'The court may think different, Mr Morrison; I'm sure the court would not want to have any doubts about what precisely you mean.'

'It's not just my opinion; there are many more professionals involved in the case; the case conference was unanimous in saying the children were being emotionally abused and neglected.'

'Ah . . . but they're not here now, Mr Morrison; we can't very well ask them can we? . . . Let us move on, Mr. Morrison . . . I see you also say in your report that you believe my client's children were being significantly harmed through . . . "psychological abuse", is that correct?'

'Yes.'

He frowned: 'psychological abuse?'

I kept my eyes on the bench; I never spoke.

'What is this . . . "psychological abuse", Mr Morrison? what does it mean?'

'Damage to the mind', I replied.

He stared at me. 'Are you a doctor, Mr Morrison?'

'No.'

'Are you a psychologist?'

'No.'

'Are you a psychiatrist?'

'No.'

'And yet you say . . . you *think* . . . my client's children were being "significantly harmed" . . . through being psychologically abused . . . you think their minds were being damaged. Do you have any proof, Mr Morrison?'

'No.'

'Do you know *what* parts of their minds were being damaged?'

'No.'

'Do you know *how* those parts of the mind were being damaged?'

'No.'

'When did you think this . . . psychological abuse took place, Mr Morrison?'

'Probably lots of times.'

'When?'

Mark's anguished expression flashed across my mind and I replied: 'when he sees his mother being attacked.'

'How often have you seen Mark seeing his mother being attacked?'

'At least once.'

'You mean once only.'

'Yes.'

'And who was doing the . . . psychological abuse, Mr Morrison, when you saw this attack?'

'Her cohabitee . . . the whole atmosphere I believe was psychologically abusive.'

'But you're not saying that my client who was being attacked was psychologically abusing her children?'

'No.'

'Are you saying her cohabitee was . . . deliberately psychologically abusing Mark when he was attacking my client?'

'I'm not saying that anybody was *deliberately* psychologically abusing the children.'

'How could it have been abuse then?'

'Because of its effects upon the children.'

'You mean causing "significant harm" . . . to their minds?'

'Yes.'

'Which you're having difficulty in explaining.'

He ignored me again, looked at his papers for the briefest moment, and continued: 'Now the other significant harm you mentioned was . . . "emotional abuse" . . . give me an example of this . . . emotional abuse Mr Morrison?'

'There are lots of ways you can emotionally abuse a child.'

'It should be easy to give me just one example then.'

'Continually shouting, rejecting the child.'

'Have you seen my client "continually shouting or rejecting"?'

'I've seen her shouting at her children lots of times.'

'And what else have you known her to do?'

'Leaving them alone at night.'

'Anything else?'

'Not giving them reassurance and physical affection when they need it.'

'Don't you have children of your own, Mr Morrison? Aren't there times they need affection and reassurance when you or your wife are not present?'

'I'm sure there are.'

'But you don't know how many times it needs to happen to warrant you calling it emotional abuse?'

'No I don't.'

The confidence was oozing away from me. I stressed that I was only one voice in a multidisciplinary team. I said: '*We* call it emotional abuse . . . when nursery staff are telling us the child is continually withdrawn and isolated, and when the health visitor and myself are finding the children left alone on numerous occasions, and when the paediatrician . . . he wrote in one of his letters to us about Mark's emotional "deadness"; it was the PAEDIATRICIAN who asked for a case conference . . . all those things . . . that's why we believe the child has been emotionally abused, when he's showing such clear signs of emotional disturbance.'

Mr Hastings' face almost lit up. 'Emotional disturbance . . .? Now is this something different from emotional abuse, Mr Morrison?'

'Yes . . . I . . . I . . . believe so. But one is the consequence of the other.'

'Can you be emotionally disturbed without being emotionally abused?'

'I would think so.'

'Are you sure, Mr Morrison? Could Mark have been emotionally disturbed and not emotionally abused?'

'Yes, I suppose he could.'

'Emotionally disturbed by something or somebody other than his mother?'

'Yes.'

'Something or somebody outside his home?'

'Yes . . . but I believe home is always more significant.'

'Oh I'm sure you do, Mr Morrison; but you will accept that this emotional disturbance you've told the court about, witnessed by the staff at the nursery, this "withdrawnness" and "isolation", may actually not be "emotional abuse", and furthermore, that it may actually not have been caused by his mother, and may not even have been caused in his home.'

'"I believe the cause of the emotional disturbance is in the home.'

'Of course you do, Mr Morrison; you believe that Mark is emotionally disturbed because he's emotionally abused in his home. Isn't that correct? Can I just check, Mr Morrison, are we talking about both children now?'

'No; I was referring to what *all* the agencies were saying about Mark.'

'I see. Their reports that he was withdrawn and isolated made you believe he was being emotionally abused. But you said in your report that you believe both children were being emotionally abused.'

'I believe the factors causing the emotional abuse of Mark are certain to have the same effect upon the younger child.'

'You mean the baby . . . the nine-month-old baby?'

'Yes.' I sensed another humiliating merry-go-round.

'So you don't believe the baby's being emotionally abused at present, but that she will be in the future?'

'I believe . . . some features of the existing situation at home do cause concern about the emotional development of Penny as well.'

'*Some features of the existing situation?* Could you be more specific?'

'I believe the mother can be . . . emotionally unresponsive to the baby.'

'Emotionally unresponsive. Do you mean she doesn't always stop everything she's doing to attend to the baby?'

'I mean more than that.'

'Can you tell the court precisely what you mean?'

'I don't believe she spends enough time with the baby; I believe the baby has too many different childminders, and too many different father-figures. These circumstances are not conducive to the child's . . . to both children's emotional . . . and psychological health.'

Mr Hastings felt no need to say any more. 'No further questions, Your Worships.' He appeared dissatisfied that the battle was over.

'You may step down Mr Morrison', said the Chair of the bench.

Mr Hastings was much more relaxed in his summing up. He gave the usual preliminaries about this 'sad case', the history of Jean's upbringing, the poverty and brutality that drove her into prostitution, the racist attacks to which she and her children were subjected; and he underlined the fact that despite all this, she somehow managed to provide for her children, never having physically abused them throughout their short lives.

'Your Worships, I have to say to you, regrettably, that Mr Morrison's testimony to this court was the worst (*he meant the best*) example of professional . . . or should I say *pseudo*-professional gobbledegook that I have ever had the misfortune to listen to.'

'You may be excused Your Worships, for asking the question why are we here at all. I would not be so arrogant as to say we should *not* be here, but as to the reason, the precise reasons my client has been accused of causing her children "significant harm" as defined in the Children Act . . . and what this harm was . . . and precisely how it was inflicted . . . I must say Your Worships, I'm completely at a loss!'

Mr Hastings did not appear or sound as though he was at a loss.

'Your Worships, my client came here today expecting to be accused of neglecting her children and determined to repudiate that accusation. But what my client could never have prepared herself for, were the offensive additional accusations made against her. And what were they? Mr Morrison has decided my client is "significantly harming" her children through something he calls . . . *emotional abuse*' (Mr Hastings gave it due emphasis and space). 'But Mr Morrison hasn't a clue what this *emotional abuse* is! Something to do, I seem to recall, with . . . *meeting emotional needs*! And if they're not met, then the child will suffer *emotional disturbance*!' His last words soared to a high pitch.

'Mr Morrison has decided my client is also "significantly harming" her children through . . . *psychological abuse*; now, whatever did he mean by that? Well, he tells us it means . . . "damage to the mind"! I'm sure you will recall me asking Mr Morrison about his authority for making such an allegation; for is it not reasonable, Your Worships, to think that if Mr Morrison accuses my client of . . . damaging the minds of her own children, a quite horrendous accusation . . . and then seeks the ultimate punishment . . . the removal of those children . . . you would think that Mr Morrison does so on reputable authority . . . WHAT AUTHORITY? NOT THE SLIGHTEST AUTHORITY, YOUR WORSHIPS . . . no medical qualification! no psychiatric qualification! Is it not a fact Your Worships, that Mr Morrison has not only failed to prove that my client is harming her children in any way, but that he has proven beyond doubt that whether he be talking about *emotional abuse, psychological abuse, emotional needs, damage to the mind, emotional disturbance, emotional deadness* . . . or any other gobbledegook you may recall . . . MR MORRISON DOES NOT HAVE A CLUE WHAT HE'S TALKING ABOUT?'

2

KNOWING OR FEELING

To 'feel' is not necessarily to 'know'

Readers may be relieved to know that the previous chapter is largely fictitious, and that it was not the author's intention to evoke memories of traumatic social work visits or painful courtroom experiences. Rather, the intention was to explore – albeit through a little humour and theatre – some of the difficulties which may arise when professionals cannot articulate the nature of specific types of 'significant harm' being inflicted upon children. Social workers will have learnt already, even though the Children Act has only recently been implemented, that it is insufficient merely to say that little Billy 'is suffering or is likely to suffer *significant harm*', section 31, etc., etc. Apart from any professional inadequacy this may constitute, courts are increasingly likely to enquire about what precisely is meant by this term: the type of harm? how it is inflicted? its immediate and long-term consequences? This book is about the emotional and psychological harm inflicted upon children by actions and behaviour which can reliably be termed 'emotional and psychological abuse'. A precondition for articulating such abuse less disastrously than our hapless imaginary colleague, is the ability to differentiate between the emotional and psychological impact which such forms of abuse have upon us. Many professionals may well think they 'know' what these terms mean, but if similarly interrogated, would quickly realize they really only have a 'feeling' that they know. Yet most child care professionals encounter emotional and psychological abuse more often than physical or sexual abuse. Knowledge and understanding depends fundamentally upon definition and explanation, and knowledge and understanding are lacking in direct proportion to the inability to define and explain.

The child protection registers which social services departments use are not particularly helpful in this regard. Some of them do offer definitions of a kind, at least for emotional abuse. But the general tendency of managers and custodians of the register is to shy away from terms like 'emotional' and 'psychological'. They much prefer the safer categories of 'physical abuse', 'sexual abuse', 'neglect' and 'failure-to-thrive', or, the most convenient catch-all category, 'grave concern'. Yet in many cases so categorized, the emotional and psychological component of the abuse may be far more significant, and if, for example, asked to define terms like 'neglect' and 'failure to thrive', and to describe what has been observed to warrant such terms, they may well find themselves describing many features of psychological and emotional abuse.

The decision to register a child under a less contentious category of abuse is taken at the end of a case conference, and has often been followed by a decision to initiate care proceedings (this sequence of events may not be so common now because of the Children Act). It is with care proceedings in mind that managers demonstrate their self-protective instincts; perhaps such instincts are more finely tuned than those of their front-line staff. Managers, and trainers too, probably realize that ad-equate definition and explanation of emotional and psychological abuse simply do not exist, and that it is extremely difficult to prove such abuse in a court of law. Legislators, particularly in the USA, know of these difficulties, and regard the matter of definitions in child care generally as a 'plague' (Smith, 1978). And there is also the possibility that those who maintain child protection registers and train social workers for child abuse work, have had similar experiences to that of the hapless colleague in the previous chapter. Little wonder they steer clear of the use of such terms. It is all a sad commentary on three decades of expansion of the child protection industry, with its accompanying increasingly more sophisticated training, and its plethora of child abuse literature.

What precisely are the difficulties?

In writing a book on the subject of emotional and psychological abuse, therefore, it is necessary at the outset to be precise about the difficulties professionals experience in both perception and feeling, and in actually coping with such abuse. First, as already implied, that neat, succinct type of definition which rolls off the tongue when, for example, we're asked about 'sexual abuse' or 'failure to thrive', does not exist in respect of emotional and psychological abuse. Secondly, there is a widely shared perception that such abuse is neither tangible nor can be proved. Thirdly, explanation and definition of these terms necessitates immersion in as yet unresolved debates in medicine and psychology; merely trying to understand 'emotion', for example, will subject one to the most incomprehensible technical and jargonistic writings (definitely not to be recommended). Fourthly, while all child care professionals will acknowledge the existence of such abuse, it is largely subsumed in their consciousness by a preoccupation with the more tangible forms of abuse. And, finally, related to the previous point, the word 'abuse' itself has been relegated in recent years; professionals are now encouraged to speak of 'child protection' rather than 'child abuse', and it is much easier to grasp the notion of protection against physical and sexual abuse than to understand the need (and the means) of protecting a child from these as yet ill-defined concepts of emotional and psychological abuse.

Each of these difficulties has to be faced. Adequate definition has to be found for the simple reason that professionals can hardly succeed in communicating with and influencing the psychologically and emotionally abusing carers if the professionals themselves are not confident in understanding and articulating the abuse. The common belief that such abuses are neither tangible nor provable is a major obstacle to being motivated to seek the right definition; that belief has got to be challenged. Whatever the degree of unresolved debate in the past about emotional and psychological development and/or abuse, we can be confident that language is flexible enough to produce a simple coherent and influential understanding of these concepts. Finally, child care professionals should accept that emotional and psychological abuse constitutes the very antithesis of every aspect of child care and development which they are employed to promote.

Surely not another book on child abuse . . .?

A wonderful cartoon appeared in a social work journal recently. A group of lofty people gathered in a circle and chattered ceaselessly. A lone individual stood at the other end of the room, painfully conscious of his exclusion. Two of the group are looking around at him rather contemptuously. One says to the other: 'he hasn't written a book on child abuse'.

Such comment implies there is enough child abuse literature. Perhaps so, but there is precious little on emotional and psychological abuse. The problem is imbalance, not saturation. Many writers have acknowledged this; Helfer and Kempe, in the first edition of their famous *The Battered Child* (1968) wrote: 'The day may come when emotional abuse can be documented readily by any physician who examines a child, but that time is not yet' (p. 186). In their third edition (1980), obviously conscious that not much progress has been made, they add the following: 'Emotional abuse *per se* is in its infancy in terms of recognition, yet it is beginning to be recognised as just as devastating as physical abuse or even more so in some situations' (p. 276).

Smith (1978), comments on the then current situation:

> The more narrow definition excludes deprivation and/or emotional abuse perhaps because of the difficulty in proving this type of abuse in court and the often conflicting interpretation of what constitutes proper emotional stimulation and home environment (p. 258).

Marginalizing emotional and psychological development

There may well be difficulty in proving that a child is being emotionally or psychologically abused, but the more fundamental difficulty for professionals is to accept that such abuse is not merely a consequence nor an appendage of the more tangible physical or sexual abuse. Professionals in case conferences spend only a fraction of the time on the psychological and emotional aspects of the child's development as they do on the alleged physical and sexual abuse which invariably has brought them together; and such discussion will usually only follow confirmation that the child has been abused sexually or physically. I recall a very typical case conference, when my colleagues and I fell into this trap.

A six-year-old child complained about pain and discomfort each time she urinated. Vaginal warts were found by the paediatrician and sexual abuse was suspected. An investigation took place and a case conference was held. Every observation and comment made by the considerable number of professionals about the family of this child, and about the child's social, emotional, psychological and educational life, was favourable; the child was progressing satisfactorily, in the home, school and community. It took only a very brief period of time to establish this point, and there was not a single doubt or dissenting voice on the matter. When the paediatrician spoke about the vaginal warts, however, a reverential silence descended upon us. This was not due to any sense of arrogance on his part; on the contrary, after a prolonged and detailed descriptive account of the case in particular, and vaginal warts in general, he told us that research in this area was not very advanced, that the literature and more expert opinion he had taken the trouble to consult was least of all conclusive and that his own conclusion now was that it was no more than a 50/50 *possibility that the child had been abused*.

The paediatrician's contribution, and his riveted audience's sub-sequent questions, totally dominated the conference. The 'riveting' nature of the contribution had obviously something to do with the uncertainty as to whether the child had been sexually abused or not, and the distinct possibility that she had. The incontrovertible evidence, accepted by everyone, was that this child was otherwise happy and content. Her social, emotional, psychological and educational develop-ment was progressing satisfactorily, and the reasons for this clearly lay in the quality of care and in the love provided for her by her parents. But these factors were of much less interest to conference participants. Nor would there have been any significant difference in the time spent on these aspects of the child's development if they had been less favourable – if say, the teacher had been talking about an unhappy child, the social worker about a family that isolates the child, the health visitor about parents who fight in the presence of the child.

Such fundamentally important observations cannot compete with the compelling nature of the enquiry as to whether the child was or was not physically or sexually abused. This is quite revealing. There are still enormous hurdles in the way of achieving a balanced sense of proportion in our perceptions of allegedly abused children, and in the value we perceive in non-medical observations of the child in her own home, family, school and community. There are many times when observations of the child's emotional, social and educational life are infinitely more revealing than the often uncertain medical diagnosis that the child has or has not been physically or sexually abused. Child abuse literature and training has failed to get this message across. More specifically, the reluctance to deal with emotional and psychological abuse, both theoreti-cally and practically, has intensified.

Awareness and intentionality

The degrees of 'intention' and 'awareness' of carers who are being investigated, will require more emphasis in this text than it has received in the previous child abuse literature. There is a common assumption that abusing carers intend to abuse, and are always aware of the *physical* and *sexual* abuse they inflict upon children, but they are much less aware and intentional if they are inflicting *emotional* or *psychological* abuse. The reason why these assumptions are significant is because some prac-titioners and writers (Lourie and Stefano, 1978) believe that if carers neither intend nor are aware of the abuse they inflict upon the child, then it should not be termed 'abuse'. There is just the hint here of a convenient yet potentially damaging identification between carer and professional. That is, if I, a professional, cannot understand or articulate emotional and psychological abuse, I cannot reasonably expect my client carers to do so; how then can they be accused of abusing the child in this way? This is a rather legalistic and evidential rationale. Lawyers and judges may find some credence in it. Child care professionals should retain a little scepticism, for good reasons. First, the basic assumption that awareness and intention are characteristically present in physical abuse cases is not proven. The early and later research on physical punishment by Newsome and Newsome (1963, 1986) highlights the frequent resort to physical punishment by a sizeable proportion of parents/carers. Most child care professionals would term many of the specific punishments (and the instruments used) as constituting 'abuse'; but there is not the slightest indication in the extensive interviewing done in this research that the parents concerned either understood or shared that view. Secondly, the once predominant assumption in child sexual abuse work that mothers nearly always know when their children are being sexually abused, has been discredited (O'Hagan, 1989). And, thirdly, sexual abuse perpetrators are capable of convincing themselves that the actual crime of sexual abuse is no abuse, that they love the child, and the child loves them, etc. We should not therefore be reluctant to acknowledge the existence of emotional and psychological *abuse* because the abusers do not perceive it as abuse, or, are not aware of it.

The nature of emotional and psychological abuse

Another reason why emotional and psychological abuse have been neglected, lies within the nature of separate child abuse categories. Physical abuse, sexual abuse and neglect are essentially crisis-laden in nature and effect; they often constitute a crisis for the victim, family and workers, and, on some occasions, a major crisis for the community, quickly fuelled by the media. Emotional and psychological abuse is seldom similarly perceived. Social workers, health visitors and the police (particularly in inner-city areas) often give the impression they have time for nothing else but 'genuine child abuse crises', i.e. physical and sexual abuse, and neglect (e.g. small children left alone). Such crises demand instant responses, like computer checks, phone calls, agency contact, medical examinations and investigations. A referral about emotional or psychological abuse is unlikely to provoke a similar response. Many child care professionals are aware of these differences and regret it. Whatever difficulty they have in articulating emotional and psychological abuse, they have a fair idea of what's happening to the child. They are conscious of the widespread damage being done, the inevitable milestones, for example, of unacceptable weight loss, the decreasing levels of emotional expression, the social isolation and withdrawal, or, the child's total confusion about their lives and their carers, and their consequential escape through fantasy. Regrettably, this type of suffering, so slow and protracted, will create no stir, pose no threat of scandal nor media scrutiny, and has little political significance for the managers of child care bureaucracies. We will see, however, that emotionally and psychologically abusive actions not only cause acute pain but also generate massive crises, for victim and professional alike.

The changing legal context of abuse

If professionals who appear in court were subjected to the humiliations inflicted upon the worker in the preceding chapter, their minds would be wonderfully concentrated on the topic of emotional and psychological abuse in preparation for the next hearing. The reality, however, is that the courts are an unlikely location for intelligent debate on the subject of emotional and psychological abuse, and solicitors who represent children are seldom likely to be asking intelligent questions about it. This is partially the fault of the legislators. Prior to the Children Act, many of the laws they formulated emphasized an underlying *welfare principle*, but quickly departed from that principle to concentrate on the 'protection' of children, i.e. protection against physical and sexual abuse, and neglect. This emphasis upon protection has proved disastrous in recent years, particularly in sexual abuse investigations, in which professionals often demonstrated a near obsessive preoccupation with protecting children while ignoring other crucial aspects of the children's development (Butler Sloss, 1988; O'Hagan, 1989).

Two of those aspects of development are 'emotional' and 'psychological'. There is not the slightest understanding of either of these in child care legislation preceding 1989; indeed, the words 'emotional' and 'psychological' seldom appear. But the 1989 Children Act, rightly heralded as the most comprehensive child care legislation that the British Parliament has produced, is different in many respects, and clearly indicates that important lessons have been learnt. The welfare principle, i.e. 'the child's welfare shall be the court's paramount consideration', is prominent in section 1 of the Act. In section 1(3), there is a list of considerations which will enable magistrates to know whether or not their decisions to grant the various orders at their disposal really are in the interests of the welfare of the child. Some of these considerations are of particular relevance to this text, e.g. the child's 'physical, emotional, and educational needs', 'the likely effect on him of any change in his circumstances' and 'any harm which he is at risk of suffering'. 'Harm' is later defined in the Act (s.31(9)) as meaning 'illtreatment or the impairment of *health* or *development*'; 'health' means 'physical or mental (i.e. *psychological*) health'; and 'development' means 'physical, intellectual, emotional, social, or behavioural development'.

This breadth and precision of child care terminology and meaning implies an awareness that children can be damaged in ways other than physical and sexual abuse. In its emphasis on 'emotional' and 'mental' (i.e. psychological) development, the Act will compel practitioners, trainers, managers, solicitors and magistrates to widen their perspective on child abuse generally, and to learn how to cope with emotional and psychological abuse in particular (practitioners will now be asked to articulate on numerous aspects of these forms of abuse, and to recommend to courts how best victims of such abuse can be alleviated of its worst effects, and be protected from it in the future). There is one quote above which needs to be stressed: 'the likely effect on him of any change in his circumstances' (s.1(3)(c)); there have been many times in recent history when professionals imposed drastic changes in children's circumstances to protect them, but failed to realize the emotionally and psychologically damaging consequences of such changes. Conversely, however, professionals have often been instructed not to seek to remove children who have been suffering severe emotional and psychological abuse on the grounds that it could not be proven; the 1989 Act is actually inviting professionals to give the most comprehensive report on all aspects of a child's development, whether it can be proven or not.

The task ahead

It is now time to look ahead, to plan how formidable obstacles encountered in this chapter can be overcome. First and foremost is the task of definition. The following chapter will provide definitions of emotional and psychological abuse, based upon our understanding of emotional and psychological development. It will contest the view that 'emotional abuse' and 'psychological abuse' are synonymous, and will demonstrate that these are quite distinct forms of abuse that need to be understood as such. Chapter 4 will consider emotional and psychological abuse within a historical, global and cultural context. Such abuse is not confined within families; indeed, governments, institutions (e.g. schools, children's homes), peer groups (i.e. bullying) and professional child care staff have collectively perpetrated it on an infinitely greater scale. Chapter 5 will apply the definitions of emotional and psychological abuse to some cases. Conceptual frameworks will be provided, enabling readers to identify the damaging 'emotional' and 'psychological' impacts of the abuse. Chapter 6 will concentrate upon carers. Clearly identifiable categories of parents/carers will emerge; many of the characteristics of these particular categories, and of their community and social contexts, will be seen to be conducive to emotional and psychological abuse. Strategies for initial contact and working with these carers/parents will be provided. Chapter 7 will focus upon four categories of emotionally and psychologically abused children, i.e. infants, children of mentally ill or alcoholic parents, emotionally abused older children, and girls who have been sexually abused by their father. Strategies for initial contact, observation and assessment will be provided. The whole of Chapter 8 will concentrate upon a case history, that of a three-year-old severely abused girl. Detailed descriptive accounts of each phase of work (i.e. referral, investigation, intervention, case conference, care proceedings and re-habilitation) will be given, interspersed with relevant comment on the tasks in hand. The objective is not to describe good practice in one particular case, but to underline sound principles and practice applicable to most cases. Chapter 9 will look at the implications of what has been written for child care agencies and training establishments.

Summary and conclusion

This chapter has looked at many of the difficulties in understanding and articulating emotional and psychological abuse. Professionals realize that such abuse is widespread, yet child protection registers seldom record it, their custodians choosing to concentrate upon the less contentious physical and sexual abuse. The fundamental difficulty is that an adequate definition of these terms does not yet exist, and definition is the basis of any progress in understanding and combating. Numerous child abuse writers have already underlined the need for addressing the problem of emotional and psychological abuse, and this chapter has illustrated how professionals in child abuse case conferences may avoid the broader, but crucially significant matter of the emotional and psychological life of the child. The lack of 'awareness' and 'intentionality' on the part of carers are important contributory factors in the reluctance to acknowledge that children are being emotionally and psychologically abused, and the failure to respond to such abuse largely stems from a perception that it does not constitute a crisis, unlike physical and sexual abuse. The legislators have made much progress; the Children Act 1989 will gradually compel all professionals involved in child protection to gain greater understanding of emotional and psychological abuse. Trainers and managers will now have to address the task of preparing and supporting front-line staff in coping with it. Hopefully, this text will make some contribution.

3

DEFINITIONS OF EMOTIONAL AND PSYCHOLOGICAL ABUSE

Introduction

The task of defining emotional and psychological abuse has been obstructed by the numerous and imprecise derivatives which child care professionals and writers use to describe the condition of children they have observed, e.g. 'emotional neglect', 'psychological deprivation', 'emotional withdrawal', 'psychological unavailability', 'emotional disturbance', etc. It is necessary to scrutinize some of the most common of these derivatives (convenient and misleading as they are) and the varying definitions based upon them. Another obstacle is the entrenched belief that 'emotional' and 'psychological' abuse are synonymous. This chapter aims to explore the origin of that view, to contest it, and to seek separate definitions for each. Before doing so, it will be necessary to review some theoretical perspectives on aspects of *emotional and psychological development*.

Some difficulties in definition

Emotional abuse

The discipline of mental health has been prominent in attempting to define emotional abuse. Schmitt (1978) writes: 'severe psychopathology and disturbed behaviour' is one of the diagnostic criteria of emotional abuse, and should be 'documented by a psychiatrist . . . emotional abuse occurs in situations where the parent is floridly psychotic, and hence inadequate to care for the children; or severely depressed, and hence a danger to the children' (p. 190). Lourie and Stefano (1978) also strongly advocate the mental health perspective: 'emotional abuse and neglect *must* be defined by the mental health professional' (p. 204). Schmitt's concluding definition suggests specific behaviour or action on the part of the carer:

> The continual scapegoating and rejection of a specific child by his caretakers. Severe verbal abuse and berating is always part of the picture. Psychological terrorism is present in some cases, e.g., locking a child in dark cellars or threats of mutilation (p. 190).

Dale *et al.* (1986) do not attempt to define emotional abuse, but in describing a group of parents who as children had experienced a 'pervasive undermining *emotional abuse*', they write that:

> . . . in such situations the child would be expected to become a little mother to younger siblings or, in effect, to look after a parent. Such children develop passive and compliant personalities as part of a pseudo-maturity which involves missing out crucial childhood developmental experiences (p. 186).

Distinctions have been drawn between 'emotional abuse', 'emotional neglect' and 'emotional disturbance'. The latter is seldom defined, and is commonly seen as a consequence of the other two experiences. Whiting (1976) records some definitions emerging from community workshops: emotional neglect occurs when 'meaningful adults are unable to provide necessary nurturance, stimulation, encouragement, and protection to the child at various stages of development' (p. 2). Another definition, however, says something entirely different: 'emotional neglect is a result of subtle or blatant acts of omission or commission experienced by the child, which causes handicapping stress on the child, and is manifested in patterns of inappropriate behaviour' (p. 3). The first definition allows for the unintentional consequence of neglect by carers too poor or too oppressed to avoid it; the second implies a high level of awareness and intentionality.

The UK government's paper *Working Together* (Department of Health, 1991) makes a clear statement on emotional abuse; it is the 'actual or likely adverse effect on the emotional development and behaviour of a child caused by persistent or severe emotional ill-treatment or rejection. All abuse involves some emotional ill-treatment' (p. 49). There are a number of questions that arise. First, is it not possible for children to be emotionally abused without it causing 'severe adverse effect' on their behaviour? Secondly, what is the difference between emotional abuse and emotional ill-treatment? The basic problem here is that this is not a definition; it is merely saying that 'emotional abuse' is caused by 'emotional ill-treatment', without defining either.

These difficulties in defining emotional abuse have had a salutary effect on recent publications. Rather than persisting, as was the hope expressed by earlier child abuse writers, the tendency is often to avoid any attempt to define. Morgan (1987) suggests one reason: 'this type of abuse is nebulous because the outward signs are hazy, indistinct and obscure'; while Calam and Franchi (1989) concede:

> Emotional abuse is a yet more difficult, diffuse concept, and thus considerably more difficult to develop adequate definitions for; arguably, the task is too difficult, and practitioners need instead to find other ways of thinking about emotional abuse (p. 75).

Psychological abuse

'Psychological abuse' is a term rarely used in child abuse literature. Even less do child care staff use it to describe their observations of children who are obviously suffering abuses quite distinct from physical or sexual abuse. And yet, terms which have clear psychological undertones are being increasingly used, e.g. 'mental injury', 'psychological distancing' 'psychological deprivation', 'psychological terror', 'psychological torture' and 'psychological maltreatment'. Let us consider some of these terms:

Mental injury: reference has been made to a greater clarity about the scope of abuse in recent child care legislation. The Children Act refers to the 'ill treatment or impairment' of 'mental health'. Many US states have been more specific; in Pennsylvania, for example, with its category of 'serious mental injury', which it defines as 'a psychological condition . . . caused by acts of omission . . . which render the child chronically sick and severely anxious, agitated, depressed, socially withdrawn, psychotic, or in fear that his/her life life is threatened' (quoted from Garbarino *et al.*, 1986).

Psychological torture is a very common term in literature generally, often applied in describing the experiences of political prisoners in the enemy camp. It is in fact inappropriate in this sense, as the core meaning of 'torture' is extreme *physical* suffering inflicted by another. Child care professionals are using this term more frequently now, particularly in relation to satanic ritualistic abuse; 'torture' and 'severe mental injury' are significant features of such abuse. Walker (1984) has a less chilling definition for 'psychological torture'; it consists of 'physical attacks upon the victim's possessions, pets, plants, and loved ones'; it can lead to 'isolation, induced debility (sleep and food deprivation); monopolizing of perceptions; verbal degradation (i.e. name calling or humiliation); hypnosis, drugs to alter consciousness, threats to kill, and occasional indulgences' (quoted from Garbarino *et al.*, 1986). Many of these experiences may warrant the term 'psychological abuse', but none of them warrant the use of the word 'torture'.

Psychological terror: the word 'terror' is a more psychologically orientated term than 'torture'. Terror is one of the five major forms of what Garbarino *et al.* call 'psychological maltreatment'. They define the act of terrorizing as follows: 'the adult verbally assaults the child, creates a climate of fear, bullies and frightens the child, and makes the child believe that the world is capricious and hostile' (p. 9). The dictionary meaning of terror is 'the condition of extreme fear' created by some 'object of dread'. Such a condition, however, is not an inevitable consequence of verbal assaults, bullying or the creation of a climate of fear. Terror is the most extreme fear, inducing panic or paralysis in its victim; the perpetrators of terror and the world they create are perceived by their victims as something more than merely 'capricious and hostile'.

Psychological unavailability refers to the child's distressing consciousness of the absence of a carer who is highly significant to the child. There are many different types of unavailability, having different impacts upon different categories of children; one would therefore have to be very specific about its context, frequency, duration and effect before suggesting that it was a form of psychological abuse.

Psychological maltreatment: Garbarino *et al.* (1986) state that this is the 'concerted attack on the child's development of self and social competence . . . a pattern of psychically destructive behaviour'. The authors do not specify what kind of destruction takes place, but they are precise about the means: 1. rejecting in which the adult refuses to acknowledge the child's worth and legitimacy of the child's needs; 2. isolating: the adult cuts the child off from forming friendships, and makes the child believe that she is alone in the world; 3. terrorizing (as already described above); 4. ignoring: the adult deprives the child of essential stimulation and responsiveness, stifling emotional growth and intellectual development; 5. corrupting: the adult mis-socializes the child, stimulates the child to engage in destructive, antisocial behaviour, reinforces that deviance, and makes the child unfit for formal social experience (p. 8).

Garbarino and colleagues' book *The Psychologically Battered Child* (1986) is the first text devoted entirely to the subject of psychological abuse. Their framework, however, identifies *emotional* experiences and not the *psychically damaging experiences* which they have already identified as the core of psychological abuse/maltreatment. 'Rejecting', 'isolating', 'ignoring' and 'terrorizing' are *not* necessarily psychically damaging experiences. They may be unpleasant experiences and they are certainly emotionally laden experiences, but we need to know much more about their context and their psychical impact before we can agree that they are, as Garbarino *et al*. believe, the five principal forms of psychological abuse. Similarly, in the case material provided, Garbarino *et al*. detail what is happening to the child *emotionally*, but tell us nothing about what is happening *psychologically*.

Is emotional abuse synonymous with psychological abuse?

Why, then, is there so much confusion in the attempt to define? There are many reasons, one of which I learnt through chairing child abuse case conferences. The conference usually began with an invitation to the participants to share views on all aspects of the child's 'welfare'. This meant seeking facts and opinions on the child's physical, emotional, social, psychological and educational development. Questions about emotional and psychological development caused difficulty. And if the child was an infant less than one year old, the difficulty was exacerbated to the extent of an embarrassing silence. If the child was much older, attempts were made to enlighten those present about the child's emotional development; very seldom did anybody respond to the query about the child's psychological development. The looks of perplexity suggested what was wrong: some conference participants wondered why they were being asked about psychological development when they had already been asked about emotional development. They believed (or felt) that the two terms were synonymous and, therefore, that 'psychological abuse' was equally synonymous with 'emotional abuse'.

The essential differences between 'emotional' and 'psychological'

The word 'psychology' is derived from the Greek words *psyche*, meaning the mind, soul or spirit, and, *logos*, meaning discourse or study. Together, they give us the well-known definition of psychology: the study of the mind, or, the science of mental life. The word 'emotion' derives from the French word *emouvoir*, meaning 'excite, move the feelings of'. Whatever interchangeability professionals have been exercising between the various derivatives of these two words, it is quite clear that their origins and meanings are different. Emotion is about feeling; 'psychological' pertains to the mind. 'Emotions set the tone of our experience and give life its vitality' (Gross, 1987, p. 5). There are many emotions – for example, fear, anger, joy, disappointment, love, envy, despair. The ability to express emotions adequately and appropriately is a crucially important aspect of development. It is easy and common for carers to impede or impair this faculty and, if they do, significant harm is done to the child's emotional development.

The 'psychological' or mental life refers to the function and development of crucial mental processes and faculties. These include the child's developing moral sense as well as the more obvious process referred to as cognition. Cognition embraces 'all those ways in which knowledge of the world is attained, retained, and used, including attention, memory, perception, language, thinking, problem-solving, reasoning, and concept attainment' (Gross, 1987, p. 5). Cognition is fundamentally important in the psychological development and life of the child. When cognitive faculties such as those mentioned above, and/or the developing moral sense, are impeded or impaired, significant harm is being inflicted upon the child's overall psychological (or mental) development. As we will see, it is easy for carers, wittingly or unwittingly, to impede or impair cognitive faculties, and to distort or pervert the child's developing moral sense.

Psychological development (i.e. mental development) is not the same as emotional development (the Children Act makes a clear distinction between the two); nor is emotional abuse the same as psychological abuse (Jones *et al.* speaks of the 'effects of abuses in the following areas: 1. Emotional life; 2. Behaviour; 3. Mental processes . . .' p. 119). Correspondingly, the emotional life is too complex to be viewed as a mere component of the psychological life. What is not in dispute, however, is that emotional and psychological development are closely linked throughout most of one's life, perpetually impinging upon and influencing each other, ineradicably fused in the creation of what we call personality. But that may be another reason for imprecision in the task of definition.

Emotional development – emotional abuse

Emotions: The earliest indicators

Darwin (1872) was one of the earliest proponents of the view that we are innately endowed with the ability to feel and express emotion. Darwin's systematic observations of his infant son were the forerunner of widespread research on the subject in the twentieth century. Watson and Morgan (1917) suggested that we are innately endowed with three primary emotions: rage, fear and love. All other emotions eventually arise from these basic emotional substrata, and will be expressed in accordance with the environmental and parental context in which the child is reared. Bowlby (1953, 1969, 1973) supports the view that we are innately endowed with certain emotional capacities. Within his own theories, he identified the primary emotions (he refers to them as signals) as crying, orientation and smiling. Bowlby was chiefly interested in what he believed was the innate disposition of the care-giver to respond to the baby's primary emotional signals, but his theory of attachment is concerned with much more than emotional development (Aldgate, 1991).

Within moments of birth, babies behave as though they are experiencing emotion, and have the ability to make movements and facial expressions associated with emotions. The newborn can cry and look *miserable* at the same time, just like an older child or adult. Give the infant a foul-tasting medicine, and you will see an expression of uninhibited *disgust*, indicating that that's exactly how she feels. Camrus (1988) recorded a whole range of emotions and accompanying expressions (i.e. happiness, sadness, anger, distress, and surprise) in her own daughter during the first few weeks of life. Not only do infants appear to be able to experience emotion, but also, even at birth, they are capable of virtually all of the component muscle movements needed for encoding different emotion states (Oster, 1978). As the child grows older, these innate, unregulated, emotional capabilities will be influenced by parental, social and cultural factors. The expression of emotion will become less unregulated, less frequent and more discrete. For example, in the first few weeks of life, her pangs of hunger will provoke her uninhibited and uncontrollable distress cry; the slightest bump or loud noise may provoke her fear. But later, as the infant adapts to the repetitive, appropriate response of the mother to these unpleasant emotional experiences, her expectation of such responses enables her to control or at least modulate emotional expression. She may not then cry so loud or for so long, because she 'feels' that the mother will quickly respond. Child care professionals will know of many cases in which infants may resort to either of two extremes in the absence of this prompt response on the part of the carer: they may simply cry in phases, each phase containing its own peak and trough of volume, distress and physical gesticulation; or, more ominously, the infant will submit to being ignored, and merely lie still, losing out on valuable and necessary vocal and motor activity, and emotional and physical stimulation from her carers. It is obvious here that a primary function of emotions and the expressive behaviour accompanying them (particularly facial), is communication. The newborn's and infant's emotional life is fundamentally a sophisticated signalling system providing vital information to the self and others (Ratner and Stettner, 1991). Facial expression accompanying the emotion is crucial within the signalling system. Abramson (1991) speaks of the face as 'our interface with the world', and for infants 'these facial expressions are their language' (p. 162).

Expression-to-feeling concordance

Differential emotions theory (Malatesta *et al.*, 1989) assumes that there is
an innate expression-to-feeling concordance in the young infant (e.g.
distress crying is accompanied by distress feelings). This relationship is
subject to change as the child grows older. The child will learn how to
dissociate the two, i.e. to control particular expressiveness accompanying particular emotions. But in the earliest stages, it's important for the
innate relationship between expression and feeling to exist, in order that
the carer may respond promptly and appropriately. Pain, pleasure, distress and hunger will all be accompanied by uninhibited expressive behaviour (not just facial), telling the carer that these are precisely the
feelings being experienced by the infant. The process by which the child
learns to control the accompanying expressive behaviour depends upon
physiological, cognitive and socialization developments. (These developments are, of course, largely dependent upon the overall quality of
care and facilitating environment provided for the infant.) A common
example of the infant 'taking control' of emotion through increased
physiological development is thumb-sucking, long recognized as a
means of self-soothing. Harris (1989) makes the important distinction
that in the first year of life, the infant can make much progress in responding selectively and appropriately to his or her mother's facial expression – this remains basically an emotionally reactive stance – but,
thereafter, the child quickly learns how to initiate emotion or bring
about change in another's emotion. The control of the facial musculature
to signal positive and negative emotions is usually observable in the
second year. Between the second and third years, the child may be able
to reinforce expressive behaviour by verbally articulating his or her
emotional state (e.g. 'I'm sad . . . happy, etc.') and also by understanding and manipulating the emotional states of others. Within the next
two years, the pre-schooler may even demonstrate an ability to 'neutral-
ize' expressions, e.g. put on the straight 'deadpan' face. Neither infants
nor older pre-schoolers are likely to be able to achieve 'masking', i.e.
concealing one's emotional state by an incongruent facial expression.
This is a much more complicated emotional achievement, demanding a
significant leap forward in cognitive development. The same applies for
the child to be able to conceal unpleasant emotional experiences beneath
an exterior and behaviour which denotes the opposite emotional experiences (Saarni, 1979). One interesting piece of research in this area is
worthy of note. It contests the view that girls are more emotionally expressive than boys, or, to be more precise, that girls do not master 'the
ability to uncouple expressive behaviour from feeling state' as quickly or
as effectively as boys. Van Leishout's (1975) longitudinal study of distress in infants between 18 and 24 months of age clearly demonstrated

that the girls in the study more quickly acquired this ability; some may suggest, however, that there are greater social pressures on girls to achieve this uncoupling.

A cautionary note: Cultural biases

Which children are these researchers referring to? Which family, community and location? Which country? Which race? There is little indication in this research of an awareness of the influence of social and cultural factors upon the development of the emotional life generally, and of the ability to control the accompanying expressive behaviour in particular. Child care workers in a variety of differing cultures in inner-city areas need to avoid deducing rigid, narrow principles and convictions from research which may have been severely limited in terms of the culture in which it was carried out. Numerous cultural groups would not regard 'the uncoupling' of expressive behaviour from the emotional state as any kind of developmental progress; conversely, other groups may be aided significantly in 'achieving' this uncoupling, by a culture, religion, group norms, etc., which demand it. The distinction in its most extreme form can be made in Howell's (1981) study of the Chewong, a small aboriginal tribe in Malaysia, and Rosaldo's study of the Ilongot in the Philippines. The Ilongot cultivate emotional expression; the cultivation of anger and passion (*liget*) is especially important, their expression a positive virtue. In contrast, the Chewong discourage the display of emotion. Successful hunting (which we would expect to be a great source of celebration), or misfortune like bereavement or an accident, should not provoke what we might regard as necessary and appropriate emotion; otherwise, greater misfortunes will befall the tribe. Ratner and Stettner (1991, p. 11) make the general point: 'cultural display rules . . . regulate which expressive behaviours are communicated and expected in specific circumstances and are required in the course of growing up in a particular culture'.

One further caution: research in emotional development has depended largely upon the availability and receptivity of healthy populations of children and their carers in hospital, clinical and school settings. Such populations and settings are light years away from the grinding poverty and decay of inarticulate, relatively unhealthy, fragmented families and communities in inner-city areas. It would be unwise to apply rigid milestones of development deduced from the former in any assessment of the latter. And professionals should ensure that poverty and fragmentation do not blind them to the essential characteristic of healthy emotional development, i.e. a high quality of interaction between child and carer.

The carer's response to the child's emotions and expressive behaviour

Emotional development in infancy and later childhood is largely dependent upon the quality and frequency of response from the carer. One does not need to be in the field of child care either to understand this or to observe it. It is constantly being demonstrated any day and any time where carers and children congregate. Each Sunday morning, I see a mother make dozens of emotional responses to her two pre-school children during a church service (sadly indicative of my lack of concentration on matters spiritual). Her children smile and laugh, play and get bored, fight and cry, sulk and complain, and occasionally take an interest in the service's colourful rituals. Their mother seems to have a limitless variety of facial, bodily and verbal emotional responses to all these emotions and expressive behaviours in her children. Often she makes her own emotional responses obvious, as when she gazes down on them with great *pride*, or when her facial musculature strains to conceal the *pleasure* and *amusement* she feels because of some harmless and witty exchange between them; or when her face drops to a *saddening disapproval*; or she turns her head with *embarrassment* and *irritation*; or she lifts the fallen and injured child with eyes full of *compassion*; or her eyes widen and she stares at them in *hurt* or *anger*. Each and every one of these emotional responses has meaning and effect on the children (not equally so, of course). The children in return may be *apprehensive, giggly, defiant, guilty, furious, curious* or *delighted*. As well as variety in number and type of expressive behaviours, the mother seems able to determine with considerable accuracy the appropriate level or intensity of her responses. Her children will, of course, quickly forget the disapproving glances of a few moments ago, and resort to the prohibited behaviour which provoked them; in which case, a stronger emotional response with its accompanying more emphatic expressive behaviour will be conveyed. Despite the enormous variety of emotional responses by mother, there is a clear imbalance between those emotions which are positive (e.g. pride, interest, compassion, etc.) and those which are negative (e.g. disappointment, anger, irritation, etc.). The positive far outweigh the negative, and are often disguised ('masked') beneath the negative; for example, she may look as though she is *disappointed* with their behaviour, but she is really quite *proud* of the fact that they are such beautiful children, impish and clever. Outside the church, in the nursery playground, in the supermarket, in their own home, these emotional interactions between children and mother (or any other carer), will be multiplied many times over; there will be more complex and lengthier emotional interactions, uninhibited and enriched by whatever touching, verbal and behavioural contributions the carers may choose.

Emotional abuse: A definition

To summarize, emotions and the expressive behaviour accompanying them can be seen in the newborn child. They perform vital tasks in communication, as much as they express internal states. This communication is normally in response to, or directed towards, a principal caregiver, usually the child's mother, and her emotional responses will determine the quality of attachment or bonding between them. As the child grows older, emotional expression may become more discrete, but the need for the caregivers to respond appropriately will remain paramount. 'Responding appropriately' predominantly means responding emotionally, and this provides the core of the definition of emotional abuse:

> *Emotional abuse is the sustained, repetitive,* inappropriate *emotional response to the child's expression of emotion and its accompanying expressive behaviour.*

The keywords here are 'sustained' and 'repetitive'. Many parents are capable of giving the inappropriate emotional response to their child at any given time, e.g. the child *cries* for the third time at four o'clock in the morning because she's *distressed*, and the parent yells out 'get lost!'; or the child comes through the door full of excitement and curiosity because of some project done at school, and the parent says 'yes, I'll look at it another time'. This is *not* emotional abuse. If, however, such inappropriate emotional responses are given to the child numerous times a day, every day of the week (i.e. sustained and repetitive), that does constitute emotional abuse, and the consequences will be clearly visible to all.

The appropriate emotional response from the caregiver validates the original emotional response from the child and vice versa. Over time, those same responses will have the effect of refining and modulating the child's emotional expressions, socializing them (i.e. enabling the child to integrate emotionally within peer groups in particular and social groups generally) and facilitating much greater understanding of the situation which has elicited the child's emotional expression in the first instance. The sustained, repetitive, *inappropriate* emotional response from the caregiver will discourage the child from expressing that particular emotion again, or may have the opposite effect of provoking the child into a massive amplification of the emotion, inappropriate at best, more likely dangerous. Over time, inappropriate emotional responses will seriously impair the child's socialization and social life; the child will be denied learning and experience of the increasing subtleties of emotional life; the child's understanding of the meaning of emotion will be distorted, whether it be the child's own emotion or emotional expressiveness in others. Children whom professionals repeatedly perceive as withdrawn, aggressive, 'emotionally flat', etc., most probably have experienced long periods during which they have learnt that there is too high a risk in expressing emotion; the risk of being met by *indifference*, or of being assaulted through *anger*, or of being undermined through *mockery*. Sustained and repetitive responses of negative emotions like these constitute emotional abuse, and seriously impair the child's emotional development in particular and her welfare as a whole.

Psychological development – psychological abuse

Establishing the boundaries

A useful definition of psychological abuse has to be based upon some understanding of psychological development. Psychological abuse obviously impedes normal or healthy psychological development, but what precisely is the latter? It is quite simply the sequence of progressive changes of the child's mental processes and faculties. Cognition embraces many of these, including attention, memory, perception, and recognition. Intelligence and associated thinking, problem solving and concept attainment, all need to be considered in assessing psychological development. The developing 'moral sense' and 'moral values' are also an important aspect of psychological development. So too is language. We will briefly examine some of these concepts:

Cognition refers to any and all of the various modes of knowing and understanding the world around us. It contrasts with the *affective and volitional*, i.e. the 'feeling' and 'will' aspects of the conscious life.

Intelligence: there are as many definitions of intelligence as there are controversies about intelligence tests (Verster, 1987; Richardson, 1991). But the concept is of such importance in psychological development that it is helpful to consider a number of these definitions. Here are three quoted by Gross (1987):

> . . . in intelligence there is a fundamental faculty, the impairment of which is of the utmost importance for practical life. This faculty is called judgement, otherwise called good sense, practical sense, initiative, the faculty of adapting one's self to circumstances. To judge well, to comprehend well, to reason well . . . (Binet and Simon, 1905).

> . . . the effective all round cognitive abilities to comprehend, to grasp relations and reason (Vernon, 1969).

> . . . intelligence is essentially a system of living and acting operations, i.e., a state of balance or equilibrium achieved by the person when he is able to deal adequately with the data before him. But it is

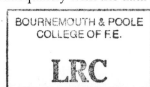

not a static state; it is dynamic in that it continually adapts itself to new environmental stimuli . . . intelligence constitutes the state of equilibrium towards which tend all the successive adaptations of a sensory, motor, and cognitive nature (Piaget, 1950).

One may refer to the first as a commonsensical definition, the second as a definition concentrating upon the intellectual aspects of the concept, and the third as focusing upon intelligence as a dynamic process. Each of them contributes to our understanding of intelligence, and allow us to reflect upon conditions, circumstances and relationships which can impair or enhance the development of intelligence. The carers who have attained some harmony in their relationship, who share decision making and the reasons underlying it with their children, who encourage and facilitate the children's exploration of the world about them, will most likely improve the children's abilities to 'comprehend, to grasp relations and reason'; or, to refer to Binet's definition, enable them to 'judge well, to comprehend well, to reason well'. Any repetitive behaviour on the part of the carer which impairs or impedes this faculty – more specifically, impairs or impedes the child's ability to make sense of the world, make it 'more simple, predictable and knowable' – is psychologically abusive.

Memory is a crucially important mental faculty upon which intelligence development and learning depend. The principal operational functions of memory are (1) registration, (2) storage and (3) retrieval of information and sensory data. A child's memory is most healthy when it is providing the optimum service to the development of faculties like intelligence, perception, language and attention. The memories of abused children in general are unlikely to provide that service; the memories of some categories of sexually abused children in particular are more likely to generate anxiety and fear which will impede development in intelligence, perception, language and attention. Some basic knowledge of memory theory would help social workers and police workers to understand the inconsistencies in children's accounts of sexual abuse. Children seldom give differing accounts of the act of abuse itself, but often give differing accounts of more peripheral matters such as the colour of hair, which knee they sat upon, which hand was used, which precise location, etc. Such consistency in respect of the central matter of the act of abuse, and such inconsistencies in respect of the more peripheral matters of context, are wholly compatible with memory theory and research, as described in Cohen *et al.* (1986). Goodman *et al.* (1991) are among the many researchers who demonstrated that 'stress was associated with enhanced memory' and 'aids consolidation of memory' (p. 145). It is ironical that abuse will somehow enhance the functioning of a mental faculty as complex as memory; yet, in so doing, it ensures the memory serves other mental processes and faculties much less than it would in the absence of abuse:

abuse may enhance the functioning of memory, but it may also impair its creative potential.

Perception is an interpretative process, interpreting the ceaseless flow of sense data we receive through all our sense organs. Gross (1987) says that it is 'the process of assembling sensations into a useable mental representation of the world . . . perception cannot occur in the absence of sensation' (p. 78); yet it is something more than sensation, and something less than comprehension. Perception 'involves the registration, recall and recognition of sensory data' (p. 79). Where there is clear recognition or identification through any of the senses, the word *apperception* is used; Winnicott (1971) comments that 'it is creative apperception more than anything else that makes the individual feel that life is worth living' (p. 76). To expose a child to safe visual, auditory and other sensory experiences, and to encourage and enable that child to explore them, identify them and to correctly associate things with them, and vice versa, is to enhance that child's faculty of perception. There is one aspect of perception crucially significant in child protection work. Healthy (acutely sensitive, discerning) perception will enhance the child's ability to protect herself from prospective abusers. This applies particularly to the older child being targeted by a sexual abuser. The child whose perception has been cultivated, is keenest and sharpest, will *sense* danger. Many at-risk children have weak perceptual powers, which make them particularly vulnerable. Vernon (1962) writes: 'the function of perception is primarily to enable [the child] to react effectively' (p. 27). Child care workers will be familiar with the numerous desensitizing environments which blunt the child's perceptual edge: the darkened rooms, the blaring television and hi-fi, the constant rowing and violence.

Language is the principal means of communication between most human beings. It affects learning, memory, thinking and socialization. Gross quotes Brown (1973), who defines it as 'an arbitrary system of symbols which taken together make it possible for a creature with limited powers of discrimination and memory, to transmit and understand an infinite variety of messages and to do this in spite of noise and distraction'. One may think language need not be considered in assessing psychological development; language is not of itself a mental process, but mental processes and faculties are instrumental in the acquisition of language. Impairment in language development may adversely affect numerous aspects of cognitive development and socialization, and it is often indicative of the quality of care of the child as a whole. There is now sufficient research evidence to demonstrate that numerous forms of maltreatment will adversely affect speech development (e.g. Allen and Oliver, 1982; Coster *et al.*, 1989).

Attention is another crucially important mental faculty which can have significant effects upon the development of nearly all aspects of cognition, particularly intelligence, memory, recognition and language. Its importance in the educational life of the child need hardly be stated. It has been defined as (1) 'the mechanisms which reject some information and take in others (whether or not the latter enters conscious awareness)' (Gross, 1987, p. 111); this is sometimes referred to as selective attention – and (2) 'as some upper limit to the amount of processing that can be performed on incoming information at any one time'. It is related to memory, and memory can easily sabotage attention and concentration. But it is not only the memory of painful experiences and the anticipation of the same which does this; many a loving carer may do precisely the same by subjecting the child to far too many (initially) pleasant experiences and stimulation. If there is not sufficient time and encouragement given to the child to learn, adapt and familiarize herself with each new experience (if she is subjected to a 'constant and unphased barrage of stimulation': Richards, 1974, p. 93), she will very quickly exhibit frustration and distress, thus minimizing her attention and concentration level. Carers who willingly afford their child time and space and demonstrate genuine interest, enjoyment and patience, are likely to enhance their child's attentive capacity. An atmosphere of relative calm within relationships and the domestic and community environment as a whole will also help. Selective attention will depend upon a strong sense of security in the child, and this in turn necessitates a pervasive sense of security and calm in the carer. Teachers are ideally placed to observe children with damaged attention faculties. Experiences like domestic strife, marital breakdowns, physical and sexual abuse are often clearly written over the nervous, sleepless faces of many classroom children. The damage done to their attention faculties, their inability to concentrate on anything except the misery they have left behind, can lead to plummeting performance levels and increased social tensions among their peer groups.

Morality: The development of a moral sense

Researchers are forever lowering the age at which they think a child is beginning to develop moral consciousness, and the age when she can think and behave in accordance with a developing moral code. There is continuous debate on how much the child's developing sense of morality is dependent upon cognitive development, and/or whether or not morality has biological roots, i.e. is the child 'biologically predisposed' to think morally (Gross, 1987) and to act morally (Harris, 1989)? We need not enter any of these interminable though fascinating debates. We need merely state that (1) moral development is a reality, (2) there is some evidence to suggest a biological predisposition towards moral thought and action, (3) the moral sense does to some extent depend upon cognitive development, specifically upon that which enables the child to see things from another's point of view (Harris, 1989), (4) there is a clear distinction between a moral consciousness having biological and cognitive roots, and that which adheres to conventions of behaviour imposed by law, custom and habit, and (5) the child's moral sense, and the thoughts and actions stemming from it, will be significant in socialization and psychological health generally.

There are different ways of impeding, distorting or corrupting the child's moral development. For example, a child can be conditioned to become violent. This may occur in a violent family, institution or peer group setting. The child may lose all sense of the immorality of violence, and lose whatever biologically or cognitively based moral censure of violence she had in the first instance (children as young as three and four in normal developmental circumstances have demonstrated a remarkable discernment – including moral censure – in their reactions to various degrees of moral transgressions: Smetana, 1981). Child sexual abuse is a potent source of damage to moral development. The perpetrator may convince the child that there is nothing wrong with such abuse. The consequences for the child's social life and mental health can be devastating; the process of finding out the truth of the matter, of attempting to salvage what remains of the moral self, can be an excruciatingly painful one.

Psychological abuse: A definition

In this attempt to secure a credible definition of psychological abuse, some additional and significant factors have been established. First, psychological abuse is a reality commonly and easily perpetrated against children. Secondly, it is not synonymous with emotional abuse, though various categories of behaviour that are primarily psychologically abusive, will also be emotionally abusive to some extent, and there are nearly always some psychologically abusive consequences when a child is abused emotionally or in any other way. Thirdly, psychological abuse can be inflicted upon children only a few months old. The failure to recognize and acknowledge this latter point stems from an extremely limited perception of very young children; an unawareness of the fact that they have numerous, interrelated and interdependent, dynamic *mental* faculties and processes, each of which demands and necessitates continuous stimulation and protection, as much as does their physiological and emotional faculties.

Psychological abuse is the sustained, repetitive, inappropriate *behaviour which damages, or substantially reduces, the creative and developmental potential of crucially important mental faculties and mental processes of a child; these include intelligence, memory, recognition, perception, attention, language and moral development.*

Psychological abuse undermines the child's attempts to understand the world around her, and make it more familiar and manageable; it will confuse and/or frighten the child, and lead to a pervasive lack of confidence adversely affecting her education, general development, and socialization. Psychological abuse may include repetitive and inappropriate emotional responses to the child, e.g. aggression, indifference, mockery, terror, rejection, etc., in which case it also constitutes emotional abuse. But it is primarily psychological abuse when it has the effect described in the definition above, i.e. damaging or substantially reducing the creative and developmental potential of mental faculties and processes. 'It is the psychological consequences of an act which define that act as abusive' (Garbarino *et al.*, 1986). The psychologically abused child may reveal a pervasive unhappiness, and/or fear, and/or distress, and a decreasing or static trend in her work performance, attentiveness, language, memory or intelligence. Her thoughts (as expressed in writing, art and play) and her behaviour may be perceived by many as serious moral transgressions.

Summary and conclusions

The length of this chapter has been dictated by some confusion generated on the subject of emotional and psychological abuse. A good starting point in attempting to understand these terms is to review the literature on the meaning of emotional and psychological *development*. Observations of the emotional life of the new born and infant, and the emotional interactions between them and the principal caregiver, clearly indicate that emotional development is *not* synonymous with psychological development, nor is the former merely one aspect of the latter. Emotional development can certainly be influenced by psychological development, particularly as the child grows older. Most theories on emotional development stress the importance of the carer's appropriate emotional responses to the child. It is the repetitive, sustained, inappropriate emotional responses of the carer to the child's emotional expressions which constitutes emotional abuse. Psychological development refers to the state of health and development of crucial mental faculties and processes. These include cognition, intelligence, perception, language, memory, attention and a moral sense. Psychological abuse is any behaviour which damages or substantially reduces the creative and developmental potential of any of these faculties or processes. It undermines the child's attempts to understand the world, and make it more familiar and manageable; it may confuse and frighten, and lead to a pervasive lack of confidence adversely affecting education, general welfare and socialization.

These abuses are as much a reality as other, more easily identified types. The latter will nearly always have some emotionally and psychologically damaging consequences. For example, violence is a frightening and inappropriate emotional response to a child for whatever reason. It is emotionally and psychologically, as well as physically, abusive. Similarly, many forms of sexual abuse will also be severely damaging to the child's emotional and psychological development.

4

GLOBAL, CULTURAL AND HISTORICAL CONTEXTS

Introduction

Emotional and psychological abuse are not solely the consequence of behaviour by individual carers. This chapter aims to explore these abuses in a global, historical and cultural context. It will look briefly at the emotionally and psychologically damaging consequences of wars, ethnic conflict, enforced emigration and racial discrimination; it will also consider the same abuses in social, religious and economic trends in history, such as the Industrial Revolution, evangelism, and within the 'Hygienist' Movement of the early twentieth century. The chapter will concentrate on the recent exposure of such abuses by child care professionals – in Staffordshire (Levy and Kahan, 1991), Belfast (Hughes et al., 1986) and Cleveland (Butler-Sloss, 1988). It will also look at the emotional and psychological abuse inherent in ritual abuse, bullying and in the abuse of disabled children.

The UN Convention on the Rights of Children

In 1989, the General Assembly of the United Nations adopted a Convention on the Rights of the Child, which has since been signed by over ninety nations. Among the Rights upheld by the Convention are: the 'rights to life, survival, and development'; 'rights concerning identity';

'rights to protection from abuse, neglect, and exploitation'. It is ironical that since the adoption of this Convention, the abuses of children in wars and civil wars have continued unabated; indeed, one might say have increased and intensified. Women and children are as always in the front line. But they are no longer merely innocent victims in the wrong place at the wrong time; their victimization is often an instrument of policy – Amnesty International has exposed the widespread use of torture of children for political ends in numerous wars and conflicts. It has also exposed (much earlier than recent press interest) the torture and murder of children for purposes of 'social control'. In its August–September 1990 edition, for example, Amnesty enclosed a petition to the Brazilian Government condemning such actions perpetrated by its police force in clearing the streets of tens of thousands of homeless children in the major cities. No country, however, holds a monopoly on such abuses of children. In South Africa, Sri Lanka, Serbia, Croatia, Israel, Botswana, Liberia, Romania, Albania, Ireland, and in many of the republics of the former Soviet Union, differing ethnic, political and religious conflicts have been – and still are – responsible for the multiple abuses of countless numbers of children. In any of these conflict situations, the children who escape death are likely to suffer emotional and psychological abuse as a consequence of the violent deaths of those dearest to them. For example, the systematic murder of fathers in the presence of their children, a frequent occurrence in the Irish conflict, is psychologically damaging in the extreme (Harbinson, 1989). Emotional development, and the development of perception, intelligence, memory, language and attention cannot be but adversely affected by such experiences.

Attack on identity as a form of psychological abuse

Conflict between different ethnic or religious communities is not the only means by which they inflict emotional and psychological abuse upon their children. In the regional examples given above, the communities (and even perhaps their children) at least have a very powerful sense of identity about themselves, their history, religion and culture; indeed, it is this sense of identity which magnifies their perception of threat by the other side. An increasing sense of identity is generally compatible with psychological development, which suggests that any effective attack upon 'identity' is likely to be psychologically damaging. Attacks upon identity, and upon the race, creed, culture and language, etc., upon which identity is based, is a central goal and characteristic of racism. Attacks upon identity may take many forms. The policy of uprooting whole populations of children, attacking or undermining their language, religion, roots and culture, is a conspicuous feature of twentieth-century history. The solutions range from the delusion of 'civilizing' (i.e. providing a materially better life for the child, through institutions or well-intentioned adoptive families) to those actions which appear to verge on genocide. Taking the former, for example, the British solution to orphans over two centuries was to dispatch them to the colonies, often without reference to the family or cultural origins, and without any kind of monitoring of the 'care' provided by the families who received them. This relatively unknown chapter in British history has recently been exposed by Melville and Bean (1990); the personal testimonies repeatedly describe continuous emotional and psychological abuse (in addition to physical cruelty and neglect) and the festering problem of lack of identity. The Swiss are now grappling with the unpleasant reality that their government and voluntary organizations actively endorsed a policy with the principal aim of eliminating its large gypsy community by forcibly assimilating them within the Swiss population. South Africa's Apartheid has been served well by the periodic uprooting of whole populations that just happened to be getting too close to the whites. Albania recently dumped thousands of its families on Italy, under the guise of complaint that Italy was encouraging the exodus (Matthews, 1991). The Gulf War has exposed Iraq's periodically similarly ruthless uprooting of the Kurds. Australia's Aboriginals have long felt their identity to be under attack, principally through the forced separation of their children, who were later fostered and adopted by white families, and by being dispossessed of a land which had such cultural and spiritual significance for them. Choo (1991) also recognizes that there are emotional and psychological consequences:

> The poverty of Aboriginal children must be considered in the context of the deprivation of the whole Aboriginal community. It includes the spiritual, *psychological, emotional* and cultural loss that has come with the failure to recognise the Aboriginal's prior ownership of this land and subsequent oppression of the Aboriginal people (p. 10, my emphasis).

Emotional and psychological abuse: Some prominent historical episodes

The industrial revolution

The physical abuse of children during the industrial revolution has been well researched and documented. To my knowledge, nothing has been written about the emotional and psychological abuse to which the children were also subjected. Such abuse was inevitable given the means by which their services were acquired, and the conditions in which they worked. Most of them were commandeered by way of the workhouse or in poor parishes, transported to factories throughout the industrial centres to work a seventy-five hour week, and had to cope with their 'severance of all family ties' (Briggs, 1959, p. 61). The Children's Employment Commission of 1860 took a particular interest in the plight of chimney boys, and exposed the abduction and sale of children as young as four and five for this purpose. The severance of the children from their parents and the physical treatment which followed must have been emotionally and psychologically destructive in the extreme. Such abuses were perpetrated against thousands of children. The industrial expansion and the factories which made it possible were more than encouraged by a government blind to its perverted morality, which convinced many of its members that the factory owners and the conditions they created actually contributed to the moral growth of children!

The evangelicals

This perception of morality in inflicting suffering upon children was not confined to capitalists; the Evangelical Movement of the eighteenth and nineteenth centuries had similar perceptions. It was not motivated by profit, but it enthusiastically endorsed the view that children should suffer. Susanna Wesley, mother of John of Methodist fame, wrote (1872): 'I insist on conquering the wills of children.' She expands by extolling the virtue of whipping for this purpose, and warns of compassion or advice to the contrary: 'Let none persuade you it is cruelty to do this; it is cruelty not to do this . . .'. More relevant to this text is the psychological abuse in Janaway's attempt to keep children's souls out of hell:

> Are you willing to go to hell, to be burned with the devil and his angels? . . . O! Hell is a terrible place . . . Did you never hear of a little child that died . . . and if other children die, why may not you be sick and die? How do you know but that you may be the next child? (*A Token for Children*, 1753, quoted in Newsome and Newsome, 1963).

Considering that the mortality rate at the time was 75 per cent, one can imagine the psychological impact of this particular method of saving souls.

The 'Hygienist' Movement

The twentieth century accelerated the process of improving the conditions of the working class generally, and outlawing the exploitation of children in particular. Religious influence began to decline, particularly in respect of the fear it had previously been able to induce in the masses. For young middle-class parents and the new, novel 'childcare' in which they were becoming increasingly interested, there was a powerful replacement: the medical expert. Newsome and Newsome (1974) write:

> . . . the time was ripe, not only for a secession from religion, but for a transfer of allegiance from the other traditional reference groups of parents, away from the methods prescribed by folklore, custom, and baby's grandmother, and towards the new blessings held out by scientific mothercraft (p. 60).

Between 1920 and 1950, many educated, socially and economically privileged parents failed to see the dangers of 'scientific mothercraft'. Newsome and Newsome claim that it was in some respects the heir of the evangelicals. There is little mention of God and damnation in the writings of the hygienists, but the advice to break the will of the child by discipline and regularity, is as severe as anything proposed by the evangelicals:

> The baby who is picked up or fed whenever he cries soon becomes a veritable tyrant, and gives his mother no peace when awake; while on the other hand the infant who is fed regularly, and played with at regular times, soon finds that appeals bring no response, and so learns that most useful of all lessons, self-control, and the recognition of an authority other than his own wishes (*Mothercraft Manual*, 1928, quoted in Newsome and Newsome, 1974).

It is when the hygienists focus upon the detail of the 'childcare' they advocate, and upon the earliest signs of the *vices* which they vigorously aim to eradicate, that they and the unwitting parents begin the process of emotional abuse. To return for a moment to the definition in the previous chapter: 'the repetitive, sustained, inappropriate emotional responses of the carer' is what the hygienists in effect recommended for coping with the slightest deviation from regularity of behaviour by the child.

The impact of the moral hygienists is seldom mentioned in the history of child abuse. Yet they were responsible for the emotional abuse of many children. Newsome and Newsome remark that it it must seem extraordinary to parents today that the educated women during that era were prepared to accept the 'content of the pronouncements or the authoritarian tone in which they were made' and then actually attempted to put them in to effect, making 'valiant efforts to stifle their natural desires to cuddle their babies', or 'feed them when they were hungry, or were wracked with guilt and shame . . . when they eased his stomach pangs in the small hours with a contraband couple of ounces' (p. 61).

Emotional and psychological abuse within the modern child care system

This brief focus on some aspects of the global and historical context of child abuse is depressing; but no more so than the current revelations of emotional and psychological abuse perpetrated by child care staff. As Jones and Novak (1991) have observed, British social work journals report virtually every week on some accusation, investigation or conviction of individuals for offences against children entrusted to their care. More worrying are those cases of groups of child care workers collectively abusing children over a long period of time. Three recent enquiry reports have examined the circumstances of such abuses – in Staffordshire, Belfast and Cleveland. The remainder of this chapter will concentrate on their findings. Each of the reports are unique in respect of (1) the context in which the abuse was perpetrated, (2) the character and motivation of those responsible, (3) the age and stage of development of the children and (4) the circumstances in which disclosures of the abuse were first made. Often the abuses were distinctly 'physical' or 'sexual', as in Staffordshire and Northern Ireland (Cleveland differs significantly in that professionals were attempting to rescue children from sexual abuse); but emotional and psychological abuse was common in all three locations.

The 'pindown' experience

'Pindown' was the name adopted by a group of residential workers in a number of children's homes and family centres in Staffordshire during years 1983–9. They were responsible for providing care for numerous children perceived as difficult-to-place and difficult-to-manage. The inquiry report (Levy and Kahan, 1991) into the pindown experience traces the development of the service provided for these children. It also provides copies of the substantial written documentation describing the philosophy and practice of pindown (referred to in the report as the Pindown documents, Appendix 5, pp. 195–256). The report identifies the inadequacy of managerial oversight and the acute and pervasive shortage of qualified residential staff. While the personality and influence of one individual, Tony Latham, is repeatedly acknowledged as the driving force behind pindown, the report demonstrates that the inadequacies of management and the lack of trained staff were crucial factors in the increasing use and intensification of the pindown system. The consolidation of the system was also served by chronic shortages of basic necessities, like adequate food, bedding, proper ventilation, appropriate accommodation and medical examination (ch. 21. para. 5). Children were constantly sick, depressed and despairing, and there were numerous suicide attempts. Such physical and mental suffering, however, was perceived as being perfectly compatible with the harshness of treatment which the pindown system demanded (e.g. one worker recorded telling a fourteen year old who slashed her wrists, 'it didn't bother me what she did to herself': ch. 6, para. 48).

The potential for emotional and psychological abuse in pindown

The rules of pindown were more severe than the Naval Detention Quarters Rules 1973, and the Imprisonment and Detention (Army) Rules 1979. This revealing point was brought to the inquiry's attention by the Official Solicitor's representative (ch. 12, para. 47), and the inquiry concluded that pindown was in effect an extremely harsh form of secure accommodation, for which there was no legal authority, facility nor safeguards. The inquiry concluded that children had suffered in varying degrees:

> . . . the despair, and the potentially damaging effects of isolation, the humiliation of having to wear night clothes . . . and of having all their personal possessions removed . . . the intense frustration and boredom from the lack of communication with others, and recreation . . . Pindown contained the worst elements of institutional control: baths on admission, special clothing, strict routine, segregation and isolation . . . inappropriate bed times (ch. 22, para. 2)

The inquiry's evidence from numerous experts in child care has often been quoted. They unanimously condemned the system, and agreed it lacked a clear theoretical framework: 'a very naive implementation of an ill-digested understanding of behavioural psychology' commented one expert (ch. 12, para. 36). The pindown documents as a whole, however, reveal a more common lack of understanding, i.e. of child development in general, and 'emotional' and 'psychological' development in particular (such words are never used in the documents). Given this lack of understanding, staff could hardly be expected to be aware of the emotional and psychological damage which many of their actions may have caused. There is not the slightest indication, for example, of any awareness of the impact upon the emotional and psychological life of the child underlying the following extract, from 'Framework of Operation' (document no. 3): '. . . use the opportunity to confront and deal with the young person . . . the purpose of such intensity is to saturate the young person' (p. 224). Ironically, this intention was never fulfilled; as the inquiry notes, the major problem (and possibly the cause of much emotional and psychological harm) was that staff saw very little of the children, but, when they did, the interactions were invariably negative and destructive (ch. 12, para. 22). However naive or ignorant the documents may be, they do not lack commitment and determination. As their severity increased in terms of the harshness of treatment they demanded, so too did the conviction of those who wrote and applied them. This latter point is important – to understand the nature and extent of the abuses perpetrated within pindown, it is essential to know the thoughts and feelings, as much as the actions, of those responsible. One learns much on these matters through the daily records and individual programme planning made available to the inquiry.

Interactions between pindown staff and children

In November 1983, three absconders were returned to a residential home and subjected 'to a deliberate episode of humiliation at the hands of a residential worker' (ch. 4, para. 47). The logbook later recorded about two of the boys: 'to work. All day they moved furniture. Work their socks off! Shame they are not wearing any' (4: 47, 49). Some indication of intent and conviction is revealed in a later entry about the same boys: '. . . the special unit (i.e. pindown) is here to stay, and every time someone "visits" us they will find it harder and longer' (4: 51). The emphasis on the word 'visit' is significant: it is the first recorded entry in the inquiry report of staff meaning something entirely different to what they've stated; the 'something different' is invariably unpleasant, and the entry suggests that staff were determined to make it so. Many similar crude codings of intent are used thereafter.

In May 1984, a residential worker recorded the admission of a girl: 'she came in with a smile on her face and greeted me as though nothing out of the ordinary had happened. I made no reply to her greeting.' Later the girl tries to speak to the worker, who records: 'I ignored this.' The girl tries again and again to speak to the worker, but is repeatedly ignored. Later she is heard 'sobbing her heart out'. She asks to speak to her social worker, but is refused: she asks to speak to other residential workers and is refused. She is heard saying: 'I will go out of my head if I stay in here.' She threatens to commit suicide. She tries again to speak to the worker, but is told that 'she would be punished further if she would not comply with the rules' (5: 37). A similar series of interactions are later recorded about a nine-year-old boy: '. . . he was smiling on his way to go home, so I had words with him and threatened to make him stay and do more jobs. He went home crying' (6: 55).

In June 1984, an eleven-year-old boy was refused contact with his parents on two consecutive days. He was made to fill 162 bags with logs. Thereafter, there are very many entries which tell of similar refusals in respect of other children. Refusing contact between the children and significant persons was a persistent feature of pindown.

In December 1984, a senior worker recorded: 'Phil arrived . . . has decided that things are a little too comfortable in here for kids . . . staff could add any other nasty little jobs which need doing' (5: 84). The significance of this recording is that it sets a precedent for developments within pindown. Within the next few years, similar entries are made, each of them either criticizing the 'leniency' of the regime (even though it was blatantly becoming harsher), or demanding and specifying particular types of harshness. The most sinister was that of 1988, made by the officer in charge of one of the homes: 'Will all staff be aware that a new, even harder pindown can operate from Sunday. I do not want anyone but the immediate staff group to know where it is. Will staff be extremely careful to let residents remain ignorant. Fear of the unknown is better than fear of the known . . . So do not feel hurt if you are not directly involved and therefore kept somewhat in ignorance yourself . . . The longer [the children] are kept in fear of new pindown the better . . .' (9: 12). The sinister aspect of this thinking lies not only in the potential for psychological abuse, but, more seriously, projecting pindown as some kind of status symbol, possibly causing some staff who implemented it to feel privileged in some way, and those who did not, deprived. The report makes it obvious that certain members of staff felt good in implementing the harshest treatment within the pindown system. Records reveal numerous expressions of gratification provoked by inflicting suffering on the children. The inquiry's authors comment: 'It is a matter of regret . . . that so many were prepared to be enthusiastic practitioners of Pindown.'

The inquiry report contains abundant similar examples of emotional and psychological abuse as defined in the previous chapter. The 'repetitive and sustained inappropriate emotional responses' are enshrined in the philosophy of pindown, and are clearly spelt out in the so-called treatment programmes for each child. For those children fortunate enough to spend brief periods in pindown, the emotional harm may have been minimal; for those who spent as much as 84 consecutive days, the emotional harm may have been substantial. One child was in pindown for a total period of 127 days. Similarly with psychological abuse. It was obvious in many of the behaviours already described and their effects: despair, suicidal attempts, sleeplessness, nightmares, etc. One can be reasonably certain that such behaviours by carers did either damage or substantially' . . . reduced the creative potential of the children's mental faculties', particularly memory and perception, and probably their moral development; and there can be little doubt about the regime's capacity for 'undermining the child's attempt to understand the world around her, confusing and frightening the child, and leading to a pervasive lack of confidence . . .'.

The 'Kincora' scandal

Inquiries into child care tragedies invariably reveal that important lessons have *not* been learnt from previous enquiries. Pindown should have been exposed much earlier through publication of Justice Hughes' Report of the Committee of Enquiry into Children's Homes and Hostels in Northern Ireland (1986). Hughes' criticism, for example, of the total inadequacy of managerial monitoring and inspection is precisely the same point made by Levy and Kahan (1991) *five* years later. Whatever inspections did take place,' . . . concentrated on the physical conditions and amenities of the premises, and the staffing difficulties . . . with comparatively little time for or emphasis upon direct contact with the individual residents . . . inspections were normally undertaken in the presence of a member of staff' (Hughes, 1986, 3: 31). The origins of the Hughes inquiry lay in allegations that the residents of the 'Kincora' boys hostel in Belfast had been sexually abused by three members of staff. All three were later convicted of serious sexual offences and were imprisoned. Similar allegations were made about other residences, and further convictions followed. The terms of reference of the Hughes inquiry were substantially widened to include investigation of numerous local authority, voluntary and religious establishments.

The victims in the Hughes Inquiry Report

Infant and childhood deprivation is a common characteristic of children in residential homes (as it was in Staffordshire's pindown), but the childhood deprivations of the children and young persons who were at the centre of the Hughes inquiry were of a far greater scale: long-term institutionalization, persistent violence, special (remedial) education, illiteracy, speech impediments, little or no knowledge of parents or roots, were all characteristics in the case histories of many of the victims. This information is important for two reasons.

First, it suggests the probability that many of them had already endured varying degrees and types of emotional and psychological abuse prior to their placements; their emotional and psychological development may have been seriously impaired. The inquiry invariably makes the comment at the end of each victim's profile: 'There was no outward sign of distress or anxiety . . .'. The implication is that the persistent sexual abuse was not affecting the victims all that much, and/or that visiting social workers and inspectors did not therefore have any grounds for suspicion. What the inquiry failed to realize was the probability that many of these victims, because of severe childhood deprivations and abuse, were incapable of expressing 'distress and anxiety' appropriately. The inquiry report in its concluding pages, however, seems to acknowledge the problem:

> The consistent failure to detect distress in abused residents, for which we have not criticized individual social workers, at least gives rise to concern that their awareness and skills in this area may be inadequate . . . (ch. 13, para. 32).

Secondly, there is the possibility that the development of perception and morality had been seriously impaired in the earlier childhoods of the victims. If this was the case, then, as was demonstrated in the previous chapter, they would have been rendered far more vulnerable to the advances of the sexual abuse perpetrators who became responsible for their welfare.

The means by which the perpetrators ensnared the boys provide clear examples of emotional and psychological abuse. Corruption began almost immediately, with the phoney 'medical' and the bath to enable the perpetrator to see and handle the victim while they were naked. The victim's reaction would determine how and when other means may be brought into play, e.g. threats of beatings, actual beatings, bribes and goodies, threats of 'bad reports' that would get them sent 'to borstal'. There was the pervasive lying necessary to sustain opportunity for abuse, and there was the continuous acting out of two incompatible roles, of carer and perpetrator. Throughout the report, the many victims consistently speak of their sense of 'shame', 'guilt', 'embarrassment' and 'fear', all of which contributed to their reluctance or inability to report what was happening to them (this factor receives prominence in the inquiry's conclusions and recommendations (ch. 13. para. 1(c)). One feeling the victims did not articulate is that of 'powerlessness', but virtually every page of the inquiry report implies that they were additionally inhibited from reporting by an overwhelming sense of the power of the men who were 'caring' for them, and their perception that such men were held in high esteem by those whom they might approach to complain. For example, one boy '. . . did not confide in Mrs Wilson because she [i.e. Mrs Wilson] respected Mr Mains [one of the convicted] and would not have believed him [i.e. the boy] (ch. 3, para. 60).

At the time of writing, another major inquiry has begun into the sexual abuse of children in residential homes in Leicester. The perpetrator received a life sentence. During his trial, many of the victims recalled similar experiences to those reported in the Hughes inquiry. Two conclusions may be drawn: first, residential homes are particularly vulnerable to exploitation by staff who intend or attempt to sexually abuse the children within them; secondly, in residential homes in which children are sexually abused, it is likely that various forms of emotional and psychological abuse both precede and follow sexual abuse. As was described in the Hughes Report, emotional and psychological abuse will be used to create the opportunity for sexual abuse; then, after the sexual abuse has taken place, different types of emotional and psychological abuse will be used to ensure the victim remains silent, fearful and willing. As was made clear in both the Levy and Kahan and the Hughes Reports, the potential for emotional, psychological and sexual abuse of children in residential homes will be diminished or increased in direct proportion to the extent of regular, rigorous and effective monitoring.

Cleveland: The investigation of child sexual abuse

The increasing realization in the mid-1980s that many children were being sexually abused gave rise to a national campaign aimed at rescuing and protecting them. But the methods used were sometimes drastic, illegal, unethical and unprofessional, and were similar, both in application and effect, to various forms of emotional and psychological abuse. The Butler-Sloss inquiry (1988) explored the experiences of numerous children in Cleveland, whom professional child care and medical personnel believed were being subjected to sexual abuse within their own families. Children were removed from their families without explanation; parents were denied knowledge of their children's whereabouts and refused contact with them; children were placed in entirely inadequate accommodation and care, e.g. hospital wards, overcrowded foster homes and residential homes; they were subjected to repeated medical examinations and photographing of their genitals (sometimes being wakened late at night for this purpose; three children from one family had their genitals examined five times by a total of six paediatricians: 1: 25, p. 16).

The causes of Cleveland are a matter of continuing debate and controversy (Campbell, 1988; O'Hagan, 1989; Franklin and Parton, 1991). The abuses unwittingly and unintentionally brought about by professionals, however, have been accepted as fact, and have cost the authority dearly in terms of compensation and reputation. Whatever differing perceptions observers may have of Cleveland, one can be reasonably certain about a crucial underlying factor: common with those responsible for the implementation of pindown in Staffordshire, the testimony of professionals in the Cleveland inquiry clearly indicated that they did not understand the consequences of their actions upon the emotional and psychological development of the children they were trying to protect. 'Rescuing' children allegedly abused, by removing them suddenly from their parents, family, home, school, friends, pets and possessions, without explanation; then subjecting them to repeated questioning and medical examination, then placing them in hopelessly overcrowded and/or inadequate alternative accommodation, and refusing them contact with family members – all this was guaranteed to cause the maximum stress and confusion. The duration of these conditions and their effects varied substantially; some children were denied contact and explanation and adequate alternative care over a long period of time; there was consequently much more likelihood of emotional and psychological damage being inflicted upon them.

Regrettably, the lessons of Cleveland were forgotten by some and ignored by others. Children have since been removed from their homes in even more drastic circumstances – in the Orkney Islands and in Rochdale. Justice Brown (1991) was particularly critical of the Rochdale social workers and managers who admitted that they had not read the Cleveland Report. Rochdale's child protection service was investigated by the Social Services Inspectorate (Department of Health, 1990). It criticized the fact that the Child Protection Register did not include the categories of 'emotional abuse' and 'neglect'. On case conferences, the Inspectorate made the following observation:

> The balance of the discussion also appeared to be weighed towards establishing that the child had been harmed and that a known person was responsible, rather than attempting an informed assessment of present and continuing risk. . . .

Inquiry reports provide ample evidence of child care and child protection workers, both in fieldwork and residential care, perpetrating emotional and psychological abuse against children. The reports highlight a fundamental fact: child care professionals and managers remain too preoccupied with the physical aspects of children's development, and that they often ignore the emotional and psychological aspects. Within such neglect lies the worker's and the agency's potential for unwittingly perpetrating such abuse. Inquiry reports on how professionals respond in particular situations should have had the effect of widening workers', managers' and trainers' focus beyond this preoccupation with whether or not a child has been physically or sexually abused. As events in Rochdale and the Orkneys demonstrate, this has not always been the case. Hopefully, the Children Act may have greater impact than inquiry reports in ensuring comprehensive assessment of all aspects of the child's development.

Organized ritual abuse

Recent disclosures by children and investigations by agencies indicate the possible existence of highly organized networks of adults who attempt to ensnare children for the purpose of subjecting them to ritualistic forms of sexual abuse (Finkelhor *et al.*, 1988; Bibby, 1991; Eaton, 1991; Harper,

1991; Tate, 1991). Tate has classified and analysed differing forms of ritual abuse. Pertinent to this text is one particular definition he provides in his introduction (p. xvii, emphasis added).

> Ritual abuse is repeated physical, *emotional, mental* and spiritual assaults combined with a systematic use of symbols, ceremonies, and machinations, designed and orchestrated to attain malevolent effects.

There is much controversy revolving around the question of the prevalency of ritual abuse (Channel 4, 1992). What is indisputable, however, is the fact that (1) when such abuse has occurred (i.e. where convictions have been obtained), the details provided in court evidence are clear examples of the definitions of emotional and psychological abuse given in the previous chapter (in particular, see Finkelhor *et al.*, 1988; Tate, 1991), and (2) it is the unique organizational, ritualistic features of the abuse which causes the greatest emotional and psychological trauma and long-term effect. If individual sexual abuse perpetrators are capable of inflicting severe emotional and psychological damage upon a child (see Chapter 5, case of Caroline), then how much easier for a sophisticated, highly organized and controlling network of perpetrators to do the same. Just as their range and subtlety of methods for ensnaring a child is greater, so too is their effort and cruelty in the types of sexual, emotional and psychological abuse they inflict.

There are two categories of emotional and psychological abuse implicit in organized ritualistic abuse; the first is that which is inherent in the sexual abuse itself – sexual abuse nearly always necessitates or gives rise to emotional and psychological abuse. The second is the emotional and psychological abuse (mainly the latter) which is inflicted to ensure that the child remains ensnared and does not reveal to anyone what is happening (given the seriousness of the crime, perpetrators will spare no effort in inflicting whatever type and degree of psychological abuse is necessary to guarantee secrecy). Children have given many accounts of the psychological pressures they endured after being subjected to sexual abuse within an organized, ritualistic context. For example, one child was told that her stomach had been opened up and a bomb placed inside, which would explode the moment she disclosed (Finkelhor *et al.* 1988). A most powerful tactic, generating the maximum guilt and fear, is to coerce the victim into the abuse of other victims until such time that the former freely accepts the 'normality' of abusing the latter.

The emotional and psychological development of children is clearly impaired by numerous features of organized, ritualistic abuse. Perhaps the greatest damage is done to the development of 'perception' – the child's perception of the world around her and her perception of self. Much of the symptomatology of children subjected to this kind of abuse by multiple perpetrators indicates that they have been indoctrinated in such a way that they perceive good in evil and evil in good. For those fortunate enough to be rescued and treated, there may later be the debilitating sense, made more acute by an enhanced memory, that their whole body, mind and spirit has been nothing more than cannon fodder belonging to nobody and/or everybody.

Emotional and psychological abuse in bullying

Unlike ritual abuse, bullying has been the subject of much research, particularly in the Scandinavian countries. After the suicides of two pupils in 1982, the Norwegian Education Ministry launched a national campaign against bullying (Tattum and Lane, 1989). The results of research in Norway and elsewhere revealed an alarming prevalence of bullying in infant, junior and secondary education (Besag, 1989). The definitions upon which research has been based emphasize the 'physical', 'emotional' and/or 'psychological' abusive aspects of bullying. The descriptive accounts of bullying and its effects, given by experts, echo much of what is contained in the definitions of emotional and psychological abuse. For example, Besag writes of the victim suffering from a sense of 'degradation, humiliation and shame, in addition to intense anger and distress'. She suggests that more emphasis should be given to the 'cognitive changes' brought about in bullying: 'they begin to believe in the abusive name calling, thinking perhaps that names such as "baby", "wimp" and "idiot" must be true, for otherwise they would have been able to cope with the bullying. Their inability to cope proves that they are inferior' (p. 53). Bullying will have a major adverse impact upon the educational and social life of the child. It is usually persistent, seldom disclosed (due to the fear of the victim) and invariably leads to a sustained deterioration in the child's emotional and psychological health. Contrary to popular belief, bullying is not confined to, nor is it inevitably predominant in, schools located in inner-city deprived areas. As Walford (1989) reveals, there is a centuries old tradition of the most brutal and psychologically abusive forms of bullying in public schools. In more recent decades, racism has been expressed through bullying. Curtis (1980) charts the course of events revolving around Bob, a black pupil from London, attending a comprehensive school in Wales. His colour and speech initially provoke 'giggling and sniggering . . . spluttering noises behind their hands . . .' which eventually lead to violent attacks upon him.

There is conflicting evidence about the precise causes of bullying (Tattum and Lane, 1989), but much progress has been made in identifying children who may be at greater risk of being bullied. Characteristics such as colour, disability, apparent clumsiness, speech, sexual orientation, dress, etc., can trigger exploratory, mocking or even hostile interactions that lead eventually to persistent bullying. Griffiths (1980) describes a case in which some teachers appear to collude with the isolation and rejection of John (aged 15), a lad very confused about his sexual identity. John is found one day 'rolling on the floor, sobbing and crying' and saying he '. . . can't take it any more'. Besag's chapter on victims of bullying gives a penetrating insight into the difficulties faced by the 'slow uncoordinated' child, thus rendering her most vulnerable to stigma and labelling. Roland (1989) gives the pessimistic findings on the result of the Norwegian campaign in one particular location (Rogoland): 'one has to conclude that the problem of bullying has increased slightly . . . from 1983 to 1986' (p. 31). Be that as it may, Besag (1989) has made a major contribution in providing teachers with comprehensive and common-sensical strategies for coping with the problem.

Emotional and psychological abuse of disabled children

There are grounds for believing that disabled children are more vulnerable to abuse (Garbarino *et al.*, 1987; Morgan, 1987; Kennedy, 1988; O'Hagan, 1989). In a survey of 150 admissions of 'multi-handicapped' children to a psychiatric establishment (Ammerman *et al.*, 1989), 69 per cent were found to have suffered physical abuse, 45 per cent neglect, 52 per cent multiple forms of maltreatment and 36 per cent sexual abuse (two-thirds of which involved penetration). Residential care is no guarantee that such abuses will cease. Recent inquiry reports and court hearings have exposed similar abuses of various categories of disabled children in residential establishments. Autistic children in a Lancashire home were made to eat their own vomit (member of staff's testimony reported in the *Independent*, 4 February 1992). Deaf children once had their thumbs tied together in the playground to discourage them from communicating through sign language, and to encourage them to lip-read (Watson, 1989). Children with profound learning difficulties are being injected with powerful sedating drugs (Hubert, 1992). Teenage mentally handicapped girls are being compulsorily sterilized to avoid pregnancy. All of these abuses are likely to include or can lead to various forms and degrees of emotional and psychological abuse. Such abuse may be more damaging in its impact than that inflicted upon children without such handicaps. The emotional and psychological development of disabled children may already have been seriously impeded as a consequence of their handicap, and the emotional and psychological stage of development which they have attained may be very fragile for the same reason.

The emotional and psychological abuse of disabled children takes precisely the same form as described in the definition. If the carer is repeatedly giving inappropriate emotional responses, e.g. shouting, aggression, contempt, mocking, ignoring, etc., the distress caused may be greatly exacerbated by the nature of the disability, e.g. deafness, blindness, paralysis, mental handicap. It is, of course, the stresses associated with caring for disabled children that can generate the emotionally abusive interactions: 'the parent/child relationship becoming enmeshed in a negative cycle that leads to abuse or progressive withdrawal' (Garbarino *et al.*, 1987, p. 11). Garbarino *et al.* emphasize that the handicapped child needs more empathy, not less. Similarly, for children with a limited understanding in particular, it will be much easier for carers to act in such a way that minimizes that already limited understanding of the world and adults around them, and to confuse and frighten them, undermining their lack of confidence even further.

Research into the abuse of disabled children is in its infancy and the initial findings are not entirely consistent; for example, Benedict *et al.* (1990) suggest that 'contrary to prediction, the more severely disabled children appeared at *less* risk of maltreatment than the disabled children functioning at more age appropriate levels'. But there is no disputing the reality of the widespread abuse of disabled children, by primary carers and their siblings initially, then by alternative professional carers. It is not difficult to abuse them emotionally and psychologically, specifically because of the particular handicaps they may have, and because such abuse will be concomitant with other more visible abuses they may endure.

Summary and conclusions

It is not only parents who abuse children emotionally and psychologically. Nor is such abuse a recent phenomenon, confined to specific geographical areas. The UN's convention on the rights of children is in effect recognition that all forms of abuse have been, and still are, perpetrated against children throughout the world. The Industrial Revolution caused emotional and psychological abuse on a massive scale. Religious indoctrination in the eighteenth and nineteenth centuries had an obvious psychologically abusive component in its formulation. In the early part of this century, in the UK and the USA, the middle classes unwittingly perpetrated emotional and psychological abuses against their own children. More recently, many children have been emotionally and psychologically abused by child care professionals responsible for their welfare. Official inquiry reports have exposed the depths of ignorance and negligence on the part of the workers and their managers, who remain too narrowly preoccupied with only the physical aspects of children's development. Recent disclosures by children have indicated the existence of organized, ritualistic abuse which is blatantly abusive to the emotional and psychological life of the child. 'Bullying' by peer groups is another form of pervasive emotional and psychological abuse which is having profound adverse consequences on the victims' overall development, and educational attainment in particular. Disabled children are especially vulnerable to all forms of abuse by carers, professionals and institutions. Their physical or mental handicap may limit their capacity to disclose what's happening to them, and the pain and distress they suffer as a consequence of the abuse may be greatly magnified because of the handicap; such multiple difficulties are particularly conducive to impeding emotional and psychological development.

5

CASE HISTORIES

Introduction

This chapter will provide ten case histories of emotional and psychological abuse. They will be heavily disguised to retain anonymity, but the abuses are exactly as described. In each case, the essential feature of emotional and psychological abuse which is prominent in the definition, namely, its sustained repetitive nature, will be emphasized. Italics will be used in describing some of the abusive interactions. Some indication of the length of the time the abuse has been developing, and of its origins, will be provided, as will numerous observations of its existing impact upon the children's social and educational development. Together with the foundations already laid in earlier chapters, these case histories will be helpful in constructing a conceptual framework for easy reference in identifying emotional and psychological abuse.

The case of Stephen, aged 11

Stephen attended special school from an early age because of a serious speech impediment and 'behavioural difficulties'. The school makes a referral saying that they have discovered bruising on his legs and Stephen's explanation is that his father 'threw him from one end of the room to the other'. Stephen is seen by a social worker at the school and willingly repeats the explanation. The social worker feels that this is a very manufactured and rehearsed explanation, and that Stephen is concealing something else. The bruising is around the top of his legs, and warrants medical opinion. Although Stephen's mother consents to this (though she chooses not to accompany Stephen to the hospital), Stephen himself literally disintegrates at the mere suggestion of medical. He trembles violently, and cries so fearfully that he has to be physically restrained and comforted. He refuses to see a doctor, and it is some considerable time before he relents. The social worker thinks he relents more because of exhaustion after so many bouts of violent trembling and profuse, fearful crying.

On the way to the hospital, his tension increases again. The paediatrician, who discovers clear evidence of anal sexual abuse, cannot restrain himself from asking: 'Who's been at you down there?' Stephen trembles and cries again, denying all knowledge. Every attempt thereafter to ask Stephen who had sexually abused him meets with panic, fear-ridden denials and tension-relieving crying. It is decided that Stephen should not return to his home that day, a decision which he wholeheartedly accepts. During the next few days, numerous contacts with child and parents are made; the following information is provided and a comprehensive assessment completed.

Stephen's parents recently separated after a protracted violent relationship. Separation did not resolve the issues; the father's cohabiting with someone else added fuel to the flames of hatred and mutual recrimination. It gradually impinged upon, and eventually overwhelmed, all other marital considerations and responsibilities. The atmosphere in the home became poisoned with a near palpable tension; the hygiene and environmental standards both inside and outside deteriorated drastically, to the extent that the parents were reported to the environmental authorities. The stench was terrible, and the fleas and animal excrement propagated alarmingly.

Stephen was the major casualty of the marital bust-up. He could not comprehend why both of his parents became increasingly less interested in him. Their eventual resort to violence terrified him. The attacks upon his mother and the resulting bruising left him distressed for days afterwards with predictable effects on his school performance and upon his social life. His parents, despite their own limitations determined by childhood and social deprivation, had over a long time been genuinely interested in him. They had attended school functions, taken him on annual holidays, paid particular attention to his health and were conscious of the difficulties he encountered as a consequence of his speech impediment. All these positive features of his life gradually disappeared, to be replaced initially by a wearying indifference, then open hostility when either parent became paranoiac about which 'side'

Stephen was taking in the dispute. When his father left, Stephen tried to maintain contact; but he suffered for that, to the extent that he ran away from his angry mother to stay with his father; but a few days after, he would pine guiltily for his mother, then return to her, and then feel precisely the same way about his father. Stephen's teachers were alarmed by the consequences: he could not concentrate; he was totally unreceptive to the speech therapy provision in his education. He was one of the last to leave the school playground. His *intellectual* achievements within the classroom virtually ceased.

It was within this context that Stephen's older brother James began sexually abusing him. James initially relied on Stephen's curiosity, aided with the odd bribe; but when the abuse graduated to persistent buggery, *fear* proved far more effective. He *terrorized* Stephen with the threat of death (it was James who was responsible for Stephen's bruises), or, the even greater threat of exposure to his mutually violent parents and the forced removal of both of them. The parents' preoccupation with hurting each other was a convenient obstacle to their protecting Stephen. The sexual abuse became more perverse and sadistic; consequently, there were the bruises with the tell-tale imprints of the hand and fingers. Stephen's deterioration was multiple, accelerated by a loss of appetite. His teachers observed an emotional life diminished to clearly visible distress and fear. His social life and social functioning within his peer group suffered too, with his withdrawnness and misery provoking an increasing amount of bullying and stigmatizing. All the abuses were then compounded by the terror inflicted by brother James in threatening to expose him to the warring parents, or kill him, or making him responsible for the removal of both of them.

Emotional abuse of Stephen

Emotions felt or expressed by child	pleading, fear, guilt, terror, helplessness
Repetitive and sustained emotional responses of carers and others	indifference, rejection, anger, scapegoating (the insensitive behaviour of professionals in repeatedly pressurizing Stephen to say who abused him may also constitute emotional abuse)
Emotional impact and consequences	emotional life increasingly limited to negative emotional experiences, e.g. unhappiness, distress; inability to respond appropriately to positive emotions in classroom and in play; negative emotions dominate child's life, i.e. persistent misery and helplessness; child losing control of emotional expression

Psychological abuse of Stephen

Repetitive and sustained behaviour of carers and others	sudden violent conflict erupts between the parents whom he loves and depends upon; their gradual separation without explanation; father's 'betrayal' in secret cohabiting; home allowed to deteriorate appallingly (i.e. destruction of shared possessions and living space) exploitation of child as an ally; punishment of child as a friend; blackmailing, with threat of violence, accompanying horrific and damaging sexual abuse
Psychological impact and consequences	losing sense of control about himself and his fate; deepest sense of loss of his once loving parents; total confusion about marital bust-up; conflict of loyalties greatly exacerbating his confusion and misery; trapped in the realization that the sexual abuse is evil and disgusting, and the reality that neither he nor his parents can put a stop to it (brother capitalizing on the existing psychological damage being done by the parents); child's confidence and self-confidence greatly undermined; his work performance and social integration at school is adversely affected; he is subjected to bullying and stigma; the faculties of intelligence development, perception, attention and speech (which needs specialist attention) impeded to varying degrees; child loses all inclination to explore, take risks, be creative

The case of Rani, aged 1 year and 6 months

Two women, Sheila and Margaret, referred the case of Rani. Rani's mother, Pawan, aged nineteen, had requested the women to look after Rani for a few days. They said Pawan was notorious for asking *anyone* to mind Rani, then going off without leaving a contact point, and refusing or being unable to pay for the childminding when she got back. The main reason for referral, however, was allegations that Pawan ill-treated Rani to the point of cruelty: tying her to the leg of the bed, almost force-feeding her, beating her, leaving her alone in her own home for long periods, particularly at night, taking her from the home at any time but again mostly late at night, and repeatedly screaming at her. These allegations were in the main substantiated.

Pawan was an untypically wayward, adolescent, Hindu child, who lied compulsively, truanted frequently, and stole money from her well-established Hindi parents. She ran away often, and was eventually ordered never to come back, having brought shame and stigma to her family. She cohabited with a criminal who was wanted by the police for numerous serious offences of robbery with violence and possession of firearms. She became pregnant and he disappeared. She was offered a dingy tenancy in an area of the city she had never known; she desperately needed the support of her neighbours, but her deceptions and erratic lifestyle alienated her further; one by one they left her to fend for herself.

When Rani was born, Pawan increasingly left her alone, or would take her at any hour of the night to some other part of the town. She became involved in prostitution. She was called upon at any time, by members of a syndicate who provided transport; she never refused. If she could not get one of her neighbours to look after Rani, she either took the child with her or left her alone. Disowned by her parents, stigmatized within her community and alienated from most of her neighbours, Pawan began to perceive Rani as the major cause of her woes. She actually told the social worker: 'she's holding me down . . . I want to be free . . . I felt as though she was doing it [i.e. persistently crying] deliberately . . .'. Thus the increasingly inappropriate emotional responses to the child: chiefly *anger* when Rani was *distressed* or when she was perceived as being deliberately provocative; unavailable and *indifferent* when Pawan left Rani alone and *frightened*; *revengeful* and *vindictive* when Rani needed Pawan's love, joy and pride in a warm embrace (the first sight of mother and daughter together alarmed two social workers; interactions were characterized by the utmost coldness and lack of physical affection).

The main component of the psychological abuse was the lack of regularity, pattern and rhythm in the child's daily life-cycle (this wreaked havoc upon the normal rhythm of her physiological and behavioural functions, a common occurrence in infants subjected to this kind of lifestyle; disorientation is the likely consequence). Rani had no bowel control; she did not display the usual indicators of bowel movement, i.e. restlessness and vocalization; she was unable to perform many of the cognitive tasks expected of a child of the same age; her language development was that of a child six months younger; her attention ability was grossly impaired by a visible anxiety; she made no discrimination between the numerous caregivers available to her; she pined remorselessly for anyone to lift her; she had little or no interest in exploring her environment; she could not remember where toy objects had been only seconds before, or where they belonged (achieved by the average twelve-month-old infant). In addition to all this, the child had the permanent look of undernourishment and disorientation, with weary and wary eyes and thin lifeless hair.

Emotional abuse of Rani

Emotions felt or expressed by child	distress (due to hunger and *isolation*), pining, frustration, clinging (to anyone), fear
Repetitive and sustained emotional responses of mother	anger, frustration, rejection, revenge, vindictiveness, coldness, aggression
Emotional impact and consequences	emotional life chiefly negative, e.g. distress, unhappiness, helplessness, fear; no experience of positive emotions; no learning of appropriateness of emotional expression

Psychological abuse of Rani

Repetitive and sustained behaviour of carer	sudden irregular departures; leaving child alone or in the care of anyone she can find; disrupting child's daily life-cycle repeatedly; exposing child to an excessive amount of environmental change, carers, and negative stimulus; repeatedly behaving towards the child and the world around her in a way which the child cannot comprehend
Psychological impact and consequences	child constantly confused and disorientated; intelligence and language development impeded by persistent confusion, inability to concentrate, and the absence of a permanent loving carer who would verbally interact appropriately with her; child cannot acquire any confidence about herself or the world around her; ceases exploring or being curious about her environment; child increasingly helpless in some bodily and mental faculties

The case of Mark, aged 8

Mark was the only child of a single parent, Iris, aged 28. She had a history of mental illness. She had no contact with Mark's father since his birth; her parents lived 250 miles away. Iris's illness was manifest in violent mood changes, triggered by the slightest provocation. She could be sitting relaxed and smiling, speaking calmly and quietly, and then suddenly yell out in rage, thundering from one room to the next, severely testing the door hinges as she went. Mark was often unfortunate enough to be in her path; that didn't stop her; usually resorted to kicking him out of her way. A typical example of these mood changes was demonstrated when the social worker arrived just as she and Mark returned from the seaside, where they had had a wonderful time. They laughed and joked about it, and both proudly showed the social worker their seaside mementoes of shells and funfair gains. Iris opened a letter that she had picked up from the hall as she came in; it was a fine of £1.50 from the local library. She went berserk, screaming abuse at both the social worker and her son. She ranted and raved about the injustices perpetrated against her from the earliest age. Mark began crying. She neither saw nor heard him crying; she was consumed by her own rage, and any attempt by the worker to pacify her or plead on Mark's behalf intensified her rage. At one point, Mark cried out to the worker 'will you look after my mammy?'

Mark was often physically abused during these outbursts. He could not make sense of, nor predict when, his mother would behave like this. But because of the inevitability that she would, he could never relax. His pervasive underlying anxiety was heightened by his constantly being on the lookout for whatever might provoke his mother; but he invariably got it wrong. For example, because of the way that his mother reacted to the library fine, and any other bill, he became visibly anxious about 'post time'. There were few nice letters to counter his increasingly distorted perception that post time was a time of danger. On another occasion in the presence of the worker, Mark lifted the cat off the table, possibly thinking that here too was a potential for his mother's explosiveness; but his action itself provoked the onslaught, which included the insult that her cats were the only friends she had in this world. This *repetitive* behaviour on the part of his mother adversely affected his educational, emotional and social development. School staff were becoming concerned, watching the inevitable deterioration in his performance within the class. The effect upon his peer group relationships was devastating; it was painful enough being a victim of his mother's attacks, but he was far more anxious about any of his friends witnessing it; and, as one of her outbursts seemed to have been provoked by his contact with friends, the safest course of action to avoid both dangers was to have no contact!

Emotional abuse of Mark

Emotions felt or expressed by child	apprehension, fear, distress, panic, helplessness
Repetitive and sustained emotional responses of mother	fun and affection suddenly turning into rage; made more angry by child's distress and fear; profuse crying and self-pity
Emotional impact and consequences	uncertain and wary about expressing positive emotions like happiness, joy, etc.; often emotionally distraught for long periods after mother's eruption; unable to integrate and respond appropriately among peer groups; fearful of friends seeing mother 'flip her lid'

Psychological abuse of Mark

Repetitive and sustained behaviour of carer	anger and violence that child cannot comprehend: a raging preoccupation with past miseries which child knows nothing about; mother, as only carer, seen in crumbling heap of self-pity; verbally insulting and violent
Psychological impact and consequences	undermining child's cognitive development; memory, attention, perception, intelligence – all adversely affected; less creative; becoming impaired; child humiliated by verbal and physical attacks, thus confidence greatly undermined; development of phobic 'avoidance' behaviour; resort to immoral behaviour (lies, strategies, etc., to avoid friends seeing mother); relationships within peer group adversely affected

The case of Jennifer, aged 1 year and 6 months, and Paul, aged 3 months

Tracy, 21, was the mother, Matthew, 34, the father. Jennifer was referred by her grandmother (secretly); she alleged that Jennifer had been beaten and bruised by Matthew, and frequently placed in the attic when she cried. During the next six months, social work, community health, and paediatric personnel became involved. Both children were hospitalized on numerous occasions due to gastroenteritis and associated illnesses. Workers were convinced that poor standards of hygiene were responsible. Neither parent was employed. They spent much time at home watching videos. The house was invariably in darkness throughout the day. Despite the attempts to enlighten the parents about sensory deprivation, the house remained in darkness, and when the door was opened to the social worker and health visitor, Jennifer recoiled from the shock of the daylight. Neither parent responded to the attempts to enable them to communicate with their children. Both children were left for very long periods in the pram and rest buggy.

Jennifer's language development seemed impaired. She could make sounds, but could utter no distinct words, not even da-da. Her motor retardation was even more severe. She had never been encouraged to play with the developmental toys and equipment provided. Her intelligence, perception and memory were seldom stimulated. She could not pick up small objects; she was incapable of the pincer grasp of thumb and index finger; she could not keep her eye on a small toy being pulled along the floor; she could not remember where objects were placed even when placed very slowly; and she could not crawl. Her range of emotional expressions was limited to negative emotion, e.g. lethargy, helplessness and fear. She appeared terrified of falling, as though she felt she could never rise again. When she was placed with foster parents, Jennifer never cried when wakened (a common indicator of the child who learns that her distress signals are going to be ignored). When outside the foster home, she appeared mesmerized by the sights and sounds around her. Soon she was expressing a range of positive emotions, like joy and exuberance, though she displayed panic and fear when the foster mother left her even for a moment. It was quite some time before she could express negative emotion indicative of a growing independence, i.e. anger, frustration, and sulk; then came the ceaseless curiosity and determination to explore the world.

It was more difficult assessing the impact of parenting and environment upon Paul. Yet it seemed that he, too, was undergoing precisely the same type of abuses. Physical contact was restricted to the minimum. Vocal and emotional interplay between parents and child was non-existent; the child did not make many demands vocally or emotionally – eating and sleeping being the major preoccupations – and the parents were not impressed by the advice that three-month-old Paul, 'very well behaved' and 'quiet little thing', needed a little more: 'Let sleeping dogs lie' said father. The most revealing indication of this came during Paul's numerous hospitalizations. He was often left at the hospital by the parents on the flimsiest pretext, e.g. he had a cold or a cough and they were worried, he was 'chesty', he seemed to have difficulty breathing, etc. While their bringing the child to the hospital was commendable, their disappearance thereafter for periods of up to a week, was not compatible with the concern originally expressed. It was a busy inner-city ward, staffed by overworked infant/paediatric nurses, who could not afford any more time for Paul than that normally given by the parents in feeding him. Thus the major abuse – both parents' emotional and psychological unavailability.

Emotional abuse of Jennifer and Paul

Emotions felt or expressed by children	distress mainly through lack of stimulation and being left for long periods in pram and rest buggy; fear in response to father's anger and aggression because they have cried or become agitated; lethargy/disinterest due to lack of stimulation; helplessness
Repetitive and sustained emotional responses of parents	ignoring, frustration, anger; no vocal or emotional interplay; emotional absence; isolating child in attic for crying
Emotional impact and consequences	emotional development seriously impaired; children being given no opportunity or stimulus enabling them to express and develop positive emotion and learn of appropriateness of emotional expression; children appear emotionally lifeless at most times

Psychological abuse of Jennifer and Paul

Repetitive and sustained behaviour of parents	keeping children in darkness most of day; providing no intellectual, perceptual or memory stimulation; violence towards child for behaviour which child cannot control; nor can child understand reason for the violence
Psychological impact and consequences	children's intelligence, perception, memory, and language development being seriously impaired (in addition to massive motor retardation)

The case of Beverly, aged 15

Beverly's misfortunes began when her parents joined a fundamentalist religious sect. She was then 13. She was encouraged to join too, but quickly became bored and disillusioned. She thereafter had difficulty in feigning interest and enthusiasm for the daily prayer and bible learning which her parents imposed upon her. She hadn't the confidence to question or oppose her parents; the fact that both parents considered themselves 'reborn' was a momentous and frightening development for her. Her *apprehension* and *perplexity* demanded great *tolerance* and *patience* on their part; she was *repeatedly* met with *biblical quotations* and *profuse apologies* for their having deprived her so long of the 'way of the Lord'. These kinds of repetitive responses *confused* and *embarrassed* Beverly. She could not help feeling that in some way she was responsible, a feeling that the parents seemed to sense and encourage. She tried to avoid the commitments expected of her. Her efforts initially were crude; she was unwell; she was delayed at school or in the sport's hall; her friend had an accident, etc. Then they became more sophisticated and daring: she would kneel with them but with a magazine or letter from her boyfriend concealed somewhere, which she dared to read while her parents prayed aloud. She was caught out, and it seemed the heavens rained down upon her, in the guise of her father's fists, and her mother's guilt-ridden anguished cries.

Her parents then went through the usual motions of interpreting such behaviour as the presence of the devil, caused by their not trying hard enough with Beverly. 'Guilt', 'punishment' and 'repentance' were what the parents thought the Lord demanded, and they were willing to provide. If she did not submit, meals would be withheld, social life terminated, television banned, pocket money ceased, and violence against her increased. Her parents' behaviour became increasingly bizarre and contradictory; for example, they repeatedly spoke of the 'unbounding love and generosity of the Lord', yet invoked this same Lord to justify blatantly unfair treatment directed against her.

The Lord's forgiveness and compassion too were boundless, yet when the parents punished her, she sensed something different from compassion. She became more guilty and embarrassed by the behaviour of her parents. She discouraged her friends from visiting; she was increasingly denied the company of her friends, who, not knowing what was happening, labelled *her* as the 'odd' one. Her school work deteriorated; her self-confidence plummeted; her seclusion intensified, and she actually began welcoming the punishment that her parents inflicted upon her.

Beverly ended up in the social services offices, her face badly bruised, having been rescued by the police. The social worker recalls one telling moment as she accompanied Beverly to a small family group home many hours later; as they got out of the car and walked towards the building, Beverly gazed above her and said: 'I can't really believe this is happening . . . it's like a dream.' She wasn't referring to any joy or relief at being rescued; what she meant was that the abuse, primarily psychological (though emotional and physical too), had been so cruel and damaging to her, that it was simply unbelievable. The social worker believed her.

Emotional abuse of Beverly

Emotions felt or expressed by child	apprehension, embarrassment, guilt, contempt, rebellion
Repetitive and sustained emotional responses of parents	exclusive ecstatic invocation of 'The Lord'; incredulity, impatience, irritation and anger provoked by Beverly's perplexity and 'stubbornness'; intolerance that increased with Beverly's 'failure'
Emotional impact and consequences	helplessness and despair in not having any control over this momentous change in her circumstances; emotional life dominated by negative emotion, and what Beverly perceives as bogus positive emotion; her father's anger and assault makes her very angry, but this changes to doubts and guilt

Psychological abuse of Beverly

Repetitive and sustained behaviour of parents	a massive conversion leading to a drastic change in the family's way of life, in the parents' perception of, and behaviour towards, their daughter; demanding similar change in daughter which she cannot make; trying to impose a newly found faith upon Beverly who recognizes but cannot escape from its inherent hypocrisy and cruelty; inducing guilt and fear by verbal insults and perceptions which claim her failure to conform is the work of the devil

Psychological impact and consequences	Beverly is flung into confusion about herself, her parents and her world; she cannot concentrate, and her school work suffers; she accepts the increasing loss of friends and their labelling of her; she loses confidence and creativity; her love of parents turning to loathing, corrupting her, compelling her to lie and deceive and avoid

The case of Tony, aged 7

Tony was the son of Mr and Mrs Greer, who separated and divorced after protracted and bitter marital conflict. Mr Greer was awarded custody of the two older children, principally because they chose to live with him. Tony chose to remain with his mother. She came from Ireland originally, and she longed to return there whenever circumstances (i.e. finance and a welcome) would permit.

Soon after the separation, Mrs Greer's drinking habit worsened. It alienated her further from her neighbours, many of whom regarded her as responsible for the marriage bust-up. The hygiene standards in the home deteriorated rapidly. Tony had to get himself up in the morning, make whatever breakfast he could if any was available for him, and travel the three-quarters of a mile to school on his own. He loathed this freedom to do what he wanted, yet preferred that his mother, recovering from yet another drunken stupor, remained in bed well out of his sight. Neighbours were disgusted watching Tony leave the home on his own, and asked him how he was getting on. Even at this early age, he sensed their pity for him and their condemnation of his mother, and he resented both. He defended his mother saying she was 'not well'. He knew he was telling lies.

Returning in the afternoon was the worst part of the day for Tony. His mother was usually returning from the pub at the same time, and he would often see her, staggering legless from one side of the pavement to the other. She spoke to everyone she met, smiling at them or cursing them; the adults ignored her, the older teenagers mocked her, and the children laughed at her. Tony saw it all, and turned on his heels many a time, running away from her. He couldn't stand it, nor could he tolerate the thought of his own condemnation of his mother. His *shame* and his *guilt* often exploded in a *profuse weeping*, which, however necessary and relieving it was, did nothing to alleviate him of the *confusion* he felt. He could recall when his faith in his mother and his dependence upon her were rewarded. He did not know what was happing now, except that it was *frightening*, and that neither he nor his mother were in control. His mother's drunken protestations of her love for him and her sacrifices on his behalf(!) were particularly confusing to him. He learnt quickly (and sensed acutely) that whatever he felt – *misery, despair, confusion, anger,* or *happiness, joy, relief, enthusiasm* (he felt precious little of any such pleasant emotional experiences) – his mother was usually incapable of making any emotional response in return, appropriate or inappropriate.

His increasing isolation from former friends (because of his mother's drinking) further limited his emotional expression. His teachers began to describe him as 'withdrawn', 'isolated' and 'anti-social'. They were unanimous in the opinion that he was terribly unhappy, and that he was carrying enormous burdens (stress) from home to school each day. He seldom smiled or relaxed in class. He couldn't *concentrate*; his work deteriorated rapidly; so too did his social status in the group – that reached rock bottom when some of his classmates taunted him about his drunken mother and he attacked them. He came off the worse. The school staff had to admonish him, even though they had great sympathy for him. He went back home that day, bruised, lonelier and more unhappy than ever. His mother saw the bruising. She demanded to know who was responsible. He wouldn't tell her. She guessed, and went to the school the following day after her lunchtime binge, and demanded that the teachers tell her who was responsible. The headteacher tried to reason with her, but it was impossible. She became violent and was forcibly removed; then she was picked up by the police. The staff tried to shield Tony from the news, but it soon leaked out. His classmates gave him an even harder time. Social services were informed. Tony was eventually taken into care.

Emotional abuse of Tony

Emotion felt or expressed by child	shame, embarrassment, anger, disappointment, sadness, misery, despair, disgust
Repetitive and sustained emotional responses of carer	drunken emotional claptrap; drunken anger; drunken threats; drunken physical affection and protestations of love
Emotional impact and consequences	pervasive apprehension that mother will be drunk again;

persistent tension revolving around how to
avoid mother, and avoid being seen in her
company;
mother's drunkenness isolates Tony, further
diminishing the opportunity for
appropriate emotional intercourse within
his peer group

Psychological abuse of Tony

Repetitive and sustained behaviour of carer	persistent loss of control of self, home and family; creating stigma and making Tony an object of pity; humiliating Tony without realizing it; always threatening to humiliate him without realizing it
Psychological impact and consequences	Tony constantly stressed and unable to function normally and happily as he once did; confidence and self-confidence greatly undermined; school work and social life seriously affected; constant threat of humiliation minimizes attentiveness and stifles all creative faculties

The case of Brian, aged 6, Mary, aged 5, and Tom, aged 3

Jack, aged 24, was the cohabitant of the mother of these children,
Maureen, aged 27. The father of Brian and Mary, and the father of Tom,
had both left the home soon after their respective children were born.
Maureen the mother had had no further relationships with men until she
met Jack. Within two weeks of joining the family, Jack made his first
physical assault against Maureen. It followed an argument in the kitchen
about money; Maureen had told him he wasn't pulling his weight. The
argument got very heated. Maureen was more intelligent and articulate
than Jack. She verbally ran rings around him. He went for her, aiming his
fists at her mouth and her eyes. The children who had been watching the
television heard their mother screaming and came running into the
kitchen. They saw blood trickling from their mother's lips, and they all
began *crying*; Mary, the middle child, defiantly asked Jack 'what did you
do to my mummy?' The children's distress compelled Maureen to try to

calm the situation. But she sensed that Jack had no such compunction; that he had no awareness whatsoever of the children's suffering, and that he was still seething with rage. A few days later, a similar row developed, with the same results. The rows and the physical assaults became *repetitive*. The pattern of interactions beforehand were similar: disputes about 'sharing the load', 'not pulling your weight', 'what do you take me for?', etc. The attacks became more ferocious and sustained, so much so that even Maureen herself lost consciousness of the impact upon her children; she struggled under the barrage of blows merely to survive. Her children watched her, repeatedly bloodied and bruised, occasionally hospitalized. Still she returned home and allowed Jack to stay.

Maureen's emotional, psychological and physical condition deteriorated. So too did the quality of care and protection that she had always given to her children. The time she could afford them was now at a premium; for example, she just didn't seem to have the time nor the inclination to put Tom on her knee and tell him a story, or tickle him, or sing him a lullaby. Little wonder, with missing teeth and an aching jaw, with repeatedly bruised and blackened eyes. Nor could she summon much enthusiasm in response to the *enthusiasm* and *excitement* of Brian and Mary returning from school to proudly display their work, to tell her of some new exciting adventure they would be embarking upon in the days ahead. Their phases of *enthusiasm* and *excitement* reduced considerably; their *learning* suffered too, prompting the headteacher to invite Maureen to 'have a chat with him'. Brian and Tom began bedwetting; all the children's appetites were affected, particularly Tom's. The nursery he attended expressed concern. They noticed a wholesale transformation in him, for the worse; he was visibly tense, very fidgety, easily distracted, and actually became distressed when he saw some of the fathers coming into the nursery with their own children. They also noticed Maureen's bruised face, and her tenseness and embarrassment, and her quick getaway from the nursery when she left Tom there, and called again to take him away. It was all such a contrast from the *patience, good humour* and *interest* she normally showed.

Maureen and Jack continually deceived themselves that all was well, and that his attacks would never occur again. The children *felt* otherwise, and Jack's presence was a constant source of *tension* and *fear* for them. You could actually see the fear and its impact in Tom's behaviour. He sat in the kitchen on his high-chair one afternoon, having difficulty as usual digesting his food. He kept looking at his mother, and glancing at the kitchen entrance, through which Jack came and went. Jack was so gigantic to him, and so *threatening*. Tom had endured enough painful experiences now to know that the increasing volume and bitter tone in their voices and their agitated movements and gesticulations were ominous. He stopped eating altogether, his mouth still half-full of unwanted dinner. He ran over to his mother's legs and clung to them; he looked up at her *fearfully* and *beggingly*; it was as if he wanted her to rescue him from his sense of *foreboding*. Ironically, Tom's *helpless plea incensed his mother more. She realized how frightened he was and why, but she frightened him more by blaming Jack for his fear, and shouting abuse at Jack for the fear and misery he was causing the whole family.* Jack attacked her with Tom still clinging onto her legs. His tiny fingers felt the reverberations of the blows to her head. The feeling terrified him and he let go and ran to the other side of the room and watched *helplessly,* and *cried hysterically.* Brian and Mary came running into the room. It was the last straw for Mary, and she hurled herself at the back of Jack, harmlessly flailing her little arms at his massive thighs. Jack felt nothing. He had an elbow stretched across her throat; his other gripping her hair tightly. Brian could not stand the sight of his mother turning purple, and he ran from the kitchen through the hall and out into the street screaming for help. Tom choked on the half mouthful of dinner he couldn't eat.

Emotional abuse of Brian, Mary and Tom

Emotion felt or expressed by children	fear, terror, anger, sadness, helplessness, pleading
Repetitive and sustained emotional responses of carers	anger (screaming and shouting) towards each other; ignoring, indifference (due to battering); mother's emotional unavailability (hospitalized); cohabitant's blind aggression towards mother
Emotional impact and consequences	children's emotional lives become dominated by the anticipation of violence towards mother and a consequential pervasive agitation and fear; increasingly unable to feel/express positive emotion because mother increasingly incapable of responding

Psychological abuse of Brian, Mary and Tom

Repetitive and sustained behaviour of parent and cohabitant	cohabitant destroys or renders helpless and humiliated the person that the children regard as their life blood; the destruction and its consequences are frighteningly visible and audible;

the violence is totally incomprehensible to the children, though increasingly predictable;

children become exploited in vicious cycle of violence, with mother initially trying to protect children, and therefore letting cohabitant know that he can also get at her by terrifying children

Psychological impact and consequences

children's mental faculties all adversely affected by witnessing violence against their mother; violence which they cannot understand nor control; a mother who they cannot protect;

faculty of intelligence building and reasoning ability undermined by incomprehensible, destructive violence;

faculty of attentiveness diminished to zero (due to sustained uneasiness and anticipation of violence against mother when Jack is about);

children's self-confidence and its development is seriously undermined by mother unable to show as much interest and pride as she had previously;

children less curious, imaginative, creative and explorative about their world

Note: The descriptive account above is an attempt to recreate actual events on the basis of retrospective study of file notes and conversations with the mother involved; the deterioration in the children's emotional and psychological functioning is factual, as recorded by the records of the GP, health visitor, social worker and school staff. The account is consistent with various research findings, e.g. Jaffe *et al.* (1990) and Hirschberg (1990).

The case of Caroline, aged 9

Caroline's family seemed normal and happy in every respect. Her father was a social worker, her mother a nurse. There were two younger children, Ben and Teresa, aged six and four respectively. Caroline was five when Teresa was born. That was the first time she could recall the inappropriate touching by her father, when he was bathing her and her mother was in hospital giving birth. He tickled her in the genital area, and she had enjoyed it. He did the same each night, and he gently touched her genital area as he tucked her in bed later. Some time after (again when mother and the other two children were not present), his horseplay with the child included similar behaviour, with both of them fully clothed. But he manoeuvred and manipulated her into reciprocating the same action on him, i.e. rubbing and tickling him in the genital area. This coincided with strategically placed hard core pornographic magazines which she could not fail to see and with his 'casual' watching of similar material on video.

Some weeks later, just after he had presented her with her favourite chocolates, he invited Caroline to horseplay again. With her mouth full of delicious chocolate, she agreed (Caroline later recalled that every graduation of the sexual abuse was preceded by the gift of her favourite chocolates). They went to the bedroom and after lots of horseplay, they lay beside each other, her father seemingly exhausted. Again he manipulated himself in such a way that her hands touched his genital area. His penis was erect, and Caroline became inquisitive. He told her that it was a secret. She asked to see. He strung her along, making her much more inquisitive. With a combination of timing, foreplay and gifts of chocolates, father made progress towards his ultimate goal. Caroline was shown videos of children being sexually abused and seemingly enjoying it. She easily graduated to mutual masturbation and oral sex. But the turning point for her came when he attempted penetration, anally and vaginally.

Despite his step-by-step planning, including lubrication, and his assiduous endeavours in conditioning her, it was a very *painful* and *frightening* experience for her. He was intelligent enough to realize his setback, but, so close to his goal, he became *impatient, less careful* and *'caring', more insensitive* and *rougher*. He could not help being impatient with her pain, particularly when he was achieving an orgasm, and so near to complete penetration. *She recalled crying out 'Mummy!' at one point. She was seven when he eventually penetrated, and the blood flowed, and terrified her more, and she terrified him when she said she was going to tell her mummy.* All his efforts at conditioning her now seemed in vain as the pain and the trauma was so great it obliterated every memory she had of committing herself to his secret. He suddenly lost control and attacked her. *He beat her around the head and gripped her by the hair. He roared at her in a menacing voice and stared at her with eyes full of hatred and fear. She trembled uncontrollably, and promised as he demanded that she would 'never never never' tell.*

Thereafter, Caroline's physical and mental health deteriorated. Her father's Jekyll and Hyde existence and treatment towards her intensified. His attempts to resume conditioning her was a waste of time now; she simply feigned that she was happy to accept his gifts, as she was terrified of the consequences of displaying her distaste for them. The burden of *terror* and *secrecy* which he inflicted upon her began to manifest itself in various ways. The school staff noticed a sharp decline in her levels of *interest* and *attentiveness*. She ceased all sports activities in which she excelled (so it seemed, but it was the undressing and preparation for sport that Caroline could not face). Her memorizing of moments ago, or of achievements weeks before, seemed incapacitated; but her memory was a frenzy of activity in other respects. She showed no enthusiasm for future activities, which, her teachers knew, would have normally generated a good deal of enthusiasm. Her relationships and status within her peer group were adversely affected; her drawings became bizarre and depressing; her behaviour increasingly self-destructive.

Her teacher reported her attempts to penetrate her wrists with sharpened lead pencils. The school staff tried to talk to her, but she denied anything was wrong. The fact is that she had been certain that her mother would realize something was wrong, and would ask, and she would tell; but her mother noticed nothing. This apparent *blindness* to her suffering greatly *perplexed* and *frustrated* Caroline. Initially, on realizing what her father was doing, she tried 'to get in her mother's way'; believing that her mother was certain to notice something was wrong and would ask her. But her busy mother behaved as if nothing was wrong. And, on another occasion, when *incomprehension and frustration at her mother's indifference to her plight became so unbearable that she burst into tears, her mother responded: 'Oh for God's sake . . . what now?' Her mother continued with her preparation for going out that night, lamenting the fact that all her hard work in the hospital and the home was in vain, as there was still no guarantee of 'a single night's peace'.*

Emotional abuse of Caroline

Emotion felt or expressed by child	fear, shame, guilt, disgust, misery, despair, helplessness, anger, pleading/begging father to stop
Repetitive and sustained emotional responses of parents	*father*: feigned love and affection, threat, anger, ruthlessness, coldness in response to child telling him how much she is suffering and detests what he's doing *mother*: indifference, intolerance, impatience, rejection
Emotional impact and consequences	child denied relief of emotions: crying provokes mother's anger and rejection; child's own anger and resistance provokes wrath of father child's worsening fear of father and hopelessness in mother leads to intensifying helplessness and despair

Psychological abuse of Caroline

Repetitive and sustained behaviour of evil parent	father deceives, manipulates and betrays child; he totally corrupts her moral development; he eventually exposes himself as a person of evil to one who regarded him as a person of great worth; mother consistently unable to rescue child; child betrayed by mother's inability to know what's going on, and to rescue her
Psychological impact and consequences	child's self-esteem shattered; she feels immersed in filth and lies; she is confused to the point of mental turmoil; she cannot reason, or plan, or predict with confidence; nothing is certain any more, except her suffering with no prospect of escape; she cannot be attentive to anything except the anticipation of the next abuse and nightmarish memories of the past; her intellectual development and school performance is adversely affected; the incomprehensibility of why her father is abusing, and of her mother's inability to rescue her, gradually leads to Caroline blaming herself for what is being done to her: *the consequence*: self-destruction

The case of Jodie, aged 2

Jodie was taken to the GP numerous times because the health visitor and the mother were concerned about her recurring illnesses, her difficulty in eating, and the very limited gains in her height, weight and head circumference charts. There were three other children, one younger and two older. Jodie's mother Susan, aged 23, was a single parent, though she had a regular partner Jim, 25, who stayed with her on occasions. The relationship was not a stable one; they argued frequently, and Jim would hit Susan, then walk out.

Social services received a referral from the GP, asking for support for the family. Susan felt she didn't need support; she merely wanted Jodie to eat as much food as her other children, and to increase in height and weight as normally. Feeding time was becoming a time of *anxiety* and *resentment* for Susan: would Jodie eat for her this time . . . and would she vomit if she did eat? She had stopped feeding Jodie while Jim was there, as he had once said to her 'give 'er to me and I'll feed 'er!' He did so, successfully, and then cast it up to her during one of their rows. She was *habitually leaving Jodie hungry and distressed*, in the hope that when she eventually did try to feed her, she would be so hungry that she must eat. But the opposite occurred; *Jodie cried loudly in Susan's ear*, and refused to swallow the spoonfuls *agitatedly placed in her mouth*. Susan was already contrasting her trouble-free feeding of the other children with her present difficulties with Jodie. And she couldn't forget that Jodie's problem was the cause of social work involvement.

The social worker and health visitor visited. They could not find any definite cause for the recurring illnesses and the worrying height and weight gains. But they were appalled at the poor hygiene, and both felt that that could be a contributory factor. They also took a dim view of Jim, concluding that he was more of a hindrance than a help to Susan. They never spoke to him. They told Susan about the lack of hygiene and the risks of infection. She resented that, and told them she wanted help in feeding Jodie, not criticism about dirt in her home. They told her they would be visiting regularly, and would help in whatever way they could.

Jodie continued to fall below the developmental curves she had been achieving six months previously. She was referred to a paediatrician. He could find no organic cause of the problem, which was labelled for the first time as 'failure-to-thrive'. A case conference was called. Susan bitterly resented this, particularly when she was told she could not attend. There was much discussion about the awful standards of hygiene, about Susan's smoking and Jim's drinking, and Susan's resentment of advice given, but little advance was made on finding the cause of the failure-to-thrive. It was agreed that if the trend continued, she would have to be hospitalized and undergo extensive tests.

Susan was both relieved and angry about Jodie going into hospital. She wanted her child to 'get better', but she felt the child was being taken away from her more because of the state of her home and her relationship with Jim, than any illnesses or feeding difficulties. She also felt undermined, with the constant interrogation about the details of her feeding Jodie, the ingredients used, the mixing, cleansing and whatever. She always had less enthusiasm and more anxiety about feeding Jodie after the social worker and health visitor left.

Jodie lost some weight in hospital in the first few days, but then began improving dramatically. The tests proved negative; the staff still could find no reason for the failure-to-thrive. Susan visited regularly despite the difficulty of finding suitable childminders in the absence of Jim. She increasingly found it a daunting task: there was Jodie as contented as you like, often in the arms of a nurse telling her what a 'delightful bonny' she was, who gave the staff no problems at all, and who ate everything put before her. Susan chose not to feed Jodie in the hospital; the *risk of humiliation* was too great.

Jodie was discharged two weeks after admission. The social worker and health visitor visited on the same day. They both remarked on how well she looked, and Susan could sense their anxiety and expectation that the child would not look so well after a few days in her care. They emphasized again the matter of hygiene, reminding Susan that Jodie had been in a spotlessly clean environment, and would therefore be even more vulnerable 'if the place was not kept clean', and the feeding utensils sterilized after every meal. Susan felt like throwing her utensils at both of them. When they had gone, she stared at Jodie for a few minutes, convinced that nothing had changed, and that she was going to have precisely the same problems again, causing those insufferable anxiety-laden people to be on her back again. She thought about Jodie in the arms of the nurses, and Jim, and admired by all and sundry, when she herself occasionally *felt like strangling the child!*

Jodie exhibited some agitation as soon as Susan was positioning her for her first meal since discharge. She took a few spoonfuls, then refused to take any more. Susan tried to persuade her with soothing words but spoken *in a tone of mounting tension.* Jodie refused to eat. *Susan suddenly screamed at her, lifted the dish of food, and threw it at the fireplace wall.* The thick, dark brown liquid spread all over the wall, then slowly descended to the mantlepiece. *Susan screamed at Jodie again and again. The child screamed back in terror. Susan burst into tears. On the following day, Susan, with renewed determination, attempted again. She 'warned' the child after each spoonful, insisting that she swallow it. Her voice was full of threat. Jodie's eyes were full of fear. At one point, when she thought Jodie was going to empty her mouth, she actually clamped her head and lower jaw, trying to prevent her from opening her mouth. Jodie tried to wrench her head free, then panicked with the sense of choking, her face changing colour and frightening Susan. Susan let go, and Jodie vomited the few spoonfuls she had taken. Susan screamed at her, more loudly and foul-mouthed than she had ever screamed before. Jodie cried helplessly.*

Emotional abuse of Jodie

Emotion felt or expressed by child	distress, resistance (to food), anxiety, fear, crying/pleading, helplessness
Repetitive and sustained emotional responses of carers and others	impatience, irritation, anger, anxiety, agitation, ignoring, embarrassment and shame (unable to feed child); (it should be stressed that the behaviour of the professionals was responsible for many of these emotional responses by the mother)

Emotional impact and consequences	sustaining and intensifying distress; magnifying mother's sense of inadequacy; child not experiencing any positive emotions; emotional development adversely affected

Psychological abuse of Jodie

Repetitive and sustained behaviour of parents and others	deliberately not feeding child (in the hope that she will eat eventually); the child cannot understand; perceiving and treating Jodie markedly different from other children; the child cannot understand; others (professionals and cohabitant) being seen and heard by child undermining, pressurizing, humiliating and confusing mother; mother perceiving child as responsible and responding/reacting to child accordingly
Psychological impact and consequences	massive confusion and insecurity resulting from above; mother unable to stimulate and nourish child's mental faculties, like intelligence development, recognition, perception, memory, attention and language; hospitalization and return to mother leads to greater confusion and disorientation for both mother and child; child increasingly feels and understands herself to be different, less valued, more vulnerable to attack from mother; child therefore persistently agitated; child increasingly (neurotically) resistant to feeding

The case of Margaret, aged 11, June, aged 7, Vicky, aged 5 and Terry, aged 3

All four children lived with their mother in a small square in one of the city's sprawling council estates. Each of the four children had a different father, of African origin. Their mother Janet was white. There were no ethnic families where they lived, no mixed-race children, nor any parent of African, Caribbean or Asian origin. The family were periodically subjected to racist abuse. Janet took it in her stride. She was used to it, predicted it, and attacked it when it showed its ugly head. Her children were not so capable. The least little disagreement in the games they played with other children in the square could provoke a torrent of verbal racist abuse. June, the seven year old, greatly depended upon her older sister Margaret to stand up to the abuse; it often *frightened* June. Such skirmishes angered Margaret more than they hurt her, and she usually performed the dual tasks of verbally demolishing her attackers and reassuring her younger sister June. She recognized the *disturbance* and *fear* experienced by Vicky and Terry, and she would often expedite their safe return to mother. Some older children would then be enlisted by the group to take revenge on Margaret; they did this through physical attacks and racist slurs. It wasn't long before parents became involved. Janet confronted the parents. June, the seven-year-old child, was *terrified by these confrontations*. Her mother was strong and resolute, but it was the *hatred* and *threat* in the eyes of screaming men and women at her garden gate which had the deeper impact upon her. She never slept on the night after, awaiting the smash of glass, or the plastic bag of excrement through the letter box, or the sound of buckets scraping along the concrete, as 'they' hurriedly daubed the racist insults on the walls, before Janet had time to get out of her bed and stop them.

June was quickly picked out as the easiest prey by a group of three older children. They trailed behind her on her way to and from school. They spat at her from behind. They made wild animal noises. They talked of burning a particular 'house' down. Then they would run ahead to look round at her, gratified in knowing that they had distressed her. June increasingly had sleepless bedwetting nights. She could not then eat even the smallest breakfast. Her face became laden with *tension* and *fearful expectancy*. The slightest unexpected noise would make her jump with fright. More ominously, when they spat on her, and she would try to remove the remains of the foul-smelling spit before entering the classroom, she began exhibiting signs of a relieving resignation and self-pity about what was being done to her and why. She was beginning to accept not just the fact that she would be repeatedly attacked because of her colour, but also the 'normality' of the attack, the 'justification' of the attack. She was learning to hate herself not because of the suffering they inflicted upon her, but because of her colour which provoked their attacks. Her mother's strength could not counter this process; in fact her mother's 'whiteness' accelerated it.

June began losing weight and stopped growing. Instead of *tensing with fear* when they spat at her from behind, she became relaxed and passive. That provoked the children even more. But the crueller they were, the less was the emotional response in June. Both mother and teachers were initially deceived by this appearance; they were well aware of previous allegations of racist harassment, and they easily observed its impact of *fear* and *distress*. Mother had been to the school often to complain. But now June looked curiously relaxed at home and in school, and she said nothing more about the attacks. Her classroom performance told a different story. Her teacher said she 'was in another world'. She wasn't concentrating, though looked as though she was; she wasn't listening either; she seldom laughed and played; she had no *enthusiasm* for tasks at which she had excelled; she no longer had any *pride* for classroom achievements in the past.

Emotional abuse of June

Emotion felt or expressed by child	pleading (for protection), fear, distress, self-hating, indifference (to her suffering), isolation
Repetitive and sustained emotional responses (of neighbours)	racist hatred, anger, threats, humiliation, isolating, mockery
Emotional impact and consequences	child in permanent state of anxiety, fear and helplessness; child experiencing less and less positive emotions, e.g. no more pride or enthusiasm; child displays bizarre inappropriate emotional behaviour: 'accepts' cruelty and mockery passively

Psychological abuse of June

Repetitive and sustained behaviour of neighbours and children	violence/degradation (of the person, i.e. spitting, racist slogans painted on walls, mob threats, etc.); initially, this violence is incomprehensible, then the child begins to understand that it is because of her colour and origins terrorizing: attacking in the middle of the night; insulting and abusing the child's principal carer
Psychological impact and consequences	child initially in a permanent state of fear, always anticipating humiliating racist abuse and attacks;

child cannot comprehend nor endure the
        magnitude nor the nature of this abuse;
child's sense of helplessness in the face of
        this enveloping racist violence greatly
        impedes and minimizes developmental
        and creative potential of her intelligence,
        memory, perception and attention;
self-confidence and self-esteem virtually
        non-existent;
child's sense of identity transformed from a
        source of pride, to a source of fear, then
        self-loathing;
child assumes 'guilt' about her colour, and
        accepts punishment for it

Conclusion

The age of the child is a crucial variable in determining the nature and
extent of damage inflicted by particular actions. Researchers who argue
against dichotomizing between emotion and cognition (e.g. Ortony *et al.*,
1988; Ratner and Stettner, 1991) have barely considered the matter of age;
they are of course concerned only with emotional and cognitive *development*, not with actions which impair such development. Take the case of
Jennifer, aged one, and Beverly, aged thirteen. The former is abused daily
by what was termed 'emotional and psychological unavailability'; the
consequences are disastrous. Beverly's parents did the opposite; they
tried to immerse her in their conversion; had they been willing to *leave her
alone*, she may not have suffered any abuse. Though her confusion and
distress were acute, the damage done was much less than that done to
Jennifer; Beverly's personality, and her emotional and psychological
development preceding her parents' conversion, was sufficiently healthy
to enable her to withstand the worst excesses of her parents' behaviour,
or to frequently betray to friends, neighbours, teachers and others that
something was seriously wrong (which eventually led to her rescue); she
did so by various actions or mere appearance. Jennifer was helpless; the
emotional and psychological unavailability was profoundly damaging.
One cannot therefore label particular actions as either emotionally or
psychologically abusive, which is what Garbarino *et al.* (1986) have done,
i.e. rejecting, terrorizing, ignoring, isolating and corrupting. It is the
emotional and psychological impact of the action which determines
whether it is emotionally or psychologically abusive, and the impact will
be determined by numerous variables, including age and stage of
development at the time such actions are perpetrated.

6

PARENTS

Introduction

Recent public inquiries have exposed inadequacies in approaching and working with the parents of children whom professionals are trying to protect. The task of approaching and working with parents of emotionally and psychologically abused children may be even more daunting; professionals have not been confident in articulating or in proving in a court that such abuse exists. Far be it, therefore, for them to attempt to explain what is happening to the carers who may be responsible for the abuse. This chapter will focus on parents and those fulfilling a parental role. A key task is recognition and categorization. Each of the abusing parents described in the last chapter represent specific categories embracing tens of thousands of parents. Abusing parents are often projected in literature and training as isolated and exceptional in terms of their plight, danger and limitations. This chapter will demonstrate the 'ordinariness' of parents who abuse their children emotionally and psychologically. Four of the categories will be examined in more detail. The aim is a more adequate preparation for initial contact and preliminary assessment.

Vulnerable groups

A striking feature of the parents in the case histories we've seen (with the exception of the parents of June), is their lack of awareness about what is happening to their children. Each parent described represents specific vulnerable categories, who collectively are responsible for the emotional and psychological abuse of tens of thousands of children. Take the case of Brian, Mary and Tom, for example. There is nothing exceptional about the horrific nature of the emotional and psychological abuse to which they are subjected as a consequence of their mother being battered; nor is there anything exceptional about the battering itself. The problem is so rampant that nearly every police force has had to establish its own domestic violence unit. Similarly with other categories of parents represented. We need to identify them and their circumstances more precisely, in order to explore some of the characteristics conducive to the emotional and psychological abuse of the children involved. Here are some prominent groups with which child care professionals will be familiar:

1 Parents of older children locked in a bitter and violent process of separation and who exploit their children for their own ends (Stephen).
2 Young single parents disowned by their parents and community (Rani).
3 Mentally ill parent(s) (Mark).
4 Alcoholic or drug-addicted parents (Tony).
5 Battered mothers of very young children (Brian, Mary and Tom).
6 Religious fundamentalist parents (Beverly).
7 Parent(s) of children diagnosed as failure-to-thrive; such parent(s) facing enormous problems in relationships and poverty, and mis-understanding by agencies (Jodie).

There are many more categories. There are also less common examples of individual parents who abuse their children emotionally and psychologically in unusual ways, and who do not readily fit into any particular category. But we will focus on four of the categories listed above, confident that the parental contexts they represent are where the greater concentration of emotional and psychological abuse lies.

The myth of the isolated, exceptional, abusing parent

Writers and researchers spend much time on parental profiles: Reiner and Kaufman (1959) speak of 'character disorders in parents of delinquent children'; Steele and Pollock (1968) focus on the 'psychopathology of the attackers', i.e. the abusing parents; Smith *et al.* (1973) look for the 'psychiatric characteristics' of abusing parents; Conte (1982) is one of many writers who identifies the sexually abusive father's 'overpowering feelings of inadequacy, dependency and anxiety' (p. 7). Labelling parents like this accentuates their different-ness, and diagnoses them as in need of medical-psychiatric or psychological help. Thus they may be subjected to devices like the 'parental behaviour inventories' (Devereux *et al.*, 1962), the Michigan Screening Profile of Parenting (Schneider, 1982) and the Parents' Acceptance–Rejection Questionnaire (Rohner, 1980). These are recommended by Garbarino *et al.* (1986) for assessing parents who abuse their children psychologically. The parents we have categorized are unlikely to submit themselves to that type of assessment. They are *ordinary* parents in more respects than those in which they may appear to be different. There is nothing uncommon about violently separating parents, nor alcoholic or mentally-ill parents, nor teenage mothers disowned by their family and community. Yet such parents are often unwittingly extremely abusive towards their children, chiefly in emotional and psychological terms. It is the *ordinariness* of the parents and their situations described in the previous chapter which is their most striking characteristic.

Parents at war

Despite the recent concern of government and the proliferation of government-supported conciliation services, many marriages still disin-tegrate in a sea of mutual recrimination, bitterness and violence. Conciliation aims to avoid that, by engaging parents at the earliest stages of separation. Then it is possible to focus a couple's attention on the impact of their separation on the children, and to sustain that attention as the separation proceeds. In the case of Stephen's parents, however, marital difficulties have 'progressed' to an all-consuming mutual hatred and violent intent. Without some kind of intervention, neither parent is capable of realizing the damage that they are perpetrating against their son, because each parent is obsessed with inflicting the maximum amount of damage on the other. Thus the primary characteristic of such parents in terms of the impact on their children is a total lack of awareness about the daily needs of their children, and (as that case painfully illustrated) an awareness of the children's mere existence strictly in terms of what side they perceive their child to be on within their dispute. Stephen's age and his special needs are contributory and complicating factors; no doubt if he was an infant or a toddler, the parents could not so easily avoid seeing the damage they inflict, as the damage would be manifest repeatedly in cries of anguish and helplessness or clearly visible withdrawal or failure-to-thrive. It is, ironically, Stephen's emotional and psychological development secured in happier times, which enables him to control any inclination he has to cry or yell out in protest about what is being done to him. Thus the parents continue along the path of mutual destruction, blind to the victim who has no opportunity to get out of their way. Even less capable are they of noticing other dangers that their children might face, or the fact that their dispute renders the child less resistant to those dangers. In Stephen's case, it is the danger of being sexually abused within the home, but it could just have easily been crime or drug addiction outside; parents simply would not have noticed. This inability to realize what is happening to their child, manifested through indifference at best and exploitation at worst, constitutes the most conspicuous emotionally and psychologically damaging feature of this particular type of parental context.

Initial contact

Having established the 'ordinariness' of the parents and their problem, and the commonness of the abuse they perpetrate, it is obvious that such cases do not necessitate some kind of extraordinary, highly specialized intervention. Similarly, however, we can say that many typical traditional approaches may not be any more useful: a kindly offer of help and counselling by appointment is not likely to inspire either parent; nor would any attempt to engage the family as a whole be appropriate; least appropriate of all (in fact quite dangerous) would be to plan to see the parents separately. Intervention necessitates confronting the parents about what precisely is happening to their child. There should be thorough preparation for this, based upon liaison and consultation, and access to accurate recordings made by teachers and other professionals in contact with the child (e.g. school medical services, pastoral carers). The timing of initial contact is crucial. One wants the parents to be home, but one may not want the child to be home (it would be a cruel irony for workers to provoke parents into a vicious verbal attack against the child in his presence, accusing him of causing professional interference).

Two workers should be involved in initial contact. The combination of social worker and a teacher who knows both parents and child well is ideal. (In Stephen's case, the sexual abuse may lead to criminal investigation, which could actually be a powerful lever for influencing parents.) School records and staff observations should reveal to parents in language they can understand the deterioration in the child's be-haviour and performance. For example, the reports may emphasize the number of times their child has been found by the teacher, alone, crying, in the outer fringes of the school's playing area; or it might stress his uncharacteristic inability to concentrate, or enthuse about things he once excelled at. The approach may be more direct: many children of warring parents will have actually described this war to their teacher; the workers can put it back to the parents, describing the distress the child showed when telling the teacher. This joint approach and shared concerns between two principal child care agencies, backed up by official reports and numerous observations, will have a powerful initial impact upon the parents. It will briefly disrupt their cycle of mutual destruction. But it will then be exploited, either of them latching onto some memory of an action by the other which, they will allege, was the cause of this damage to the child that they are being told about. This will inevitably be followed by the partner's counter-memory and the cycle will quickly reassert itself, sabotaging the workers' intentions (and threatening to overwhelm the workers!). But it is precisely that kind of scenario which the workers need to witness, and to play back to the parents in whatever way is available to them.

I recall many instances in which I have done this, exposing *both* parents' skilful conversion of professional concern into their usual means of totally obliterating the child from their minds, namely, by wanting to kill each other! The exposure of this tactic with the clear implication that it confirms the workers' conviction about damage which is being done to the child, concentrates the mind wonderfully, and provokes much guilt (it should be stressed, however, that provoking guilt in parents can never be a legitimate objective in itself; it is merely an inevitable consequence of them recreating their own child-abusing scenario; it also contains some therapeutic potential). In the exceptional case of Stephen, where the parents' self-preoccupation has enabled the older brother to sexually abuse him with little possibility of them knowing, the exposure and the guilt consequences for the parents have enormous dangers. Such a revelation may provoke not just the usual cycle of violence between the parents, but an overwhelmingly guilt-ridden murderous attack on the brother, or possibly an equally guilt-ridden suicidal attempt by either parent. In such a case, therefore, there is the additional necessity of predicting such an outcome and carefully preparing with the police in particular the contingency plan that will present it.

Single teenage mothers: The social and economic and cultural constructs

Many child care professionals, in whichever agency they work, are likely to be reporting an increase in the number of single teenage mothers referred to them. If their parents have been tolerant and supportive throughout their pregnancies, and maintain that tolerance and support when the child is born, there is no reason at all for any childcare agency involvement beyond that statutorily provided to all pregnant women and mothers. But those who do come to the attention of agencies for other reasons are not so fortunate. Like Pawan, the mother of Rani, they may have been disowned by their parents; or the problems in their own families may have been so overwhelming that pregnancy was seen as the most convenient means of escape; or, the intention was a purely romantic notion of running away with the father of the child, only to discover painfully that the father himself has run away from the awesome realization of the responsibility of parenthood! The plight of these mothers is profoundly serious and acutely felt. Many of them cannot return. They are often homeless, penniless and friendless. They are easy prey for unscrupulous individuals. They are often offered accommodation by people whose motivation is less than benevolent, and they can then find themselves homeless again, having failed to fulfil the expectations made of them. They will be compelled to move frequently from lodgings to bedsits, from hostels to flats, from friends to distant relatives more sympathetic than their own parents. They and their children may live in a perpetual state of crisis, impermanency, disruption, hostility and rejection. They are often perceived by the community as feckless, immature, selfish, irresponsible adolescents who have nothing to offer.

Initial contact

Such parents are unlikely to have fond memories of professionals. Many of them will perceive the health visitor or social worker as a source of harassment or danger, i.e. someone who will take their child away. Perceptions of the professionals may well be an additional reason why some young single parent mothers don't stay around too long. The initial contact should be based upon an acute sensitivity to this possibility. Don't be surprised if mother doesn't turn up when she said she would, or isn't at home when you call, or is at home but won't answer. And do not let such behaviour fulfil her prophecy by adopting a more vigorous, determined strategy of getting the child into care. It is helpful to explore the mother's perceptions of previous child care professionals and other agencies, not to ingratiate oneself at the expense of casting aspersions on one's professional predecessors, but for the more simple objective of locating the greatest source of distrust or hostility the mother may harbour, and, the origins of it. This may simply have been a turn of phrase by a predecessor, a point of emphasis, a gesture, a look of real concern directed at the child, any of which was grossly misinterpreted by the mother as a determined move to remove their child. Or it may have been an action more blatant: a direct condemnation, a warning, a threat to remove. Even if mother refuses to see you, this exploration of previous contacts with professionals can and should take place through other means: the mother's former friends and relatives (friends and relatives should be seriously considered as introductory intermediaries in particularly difficult relationships between the mother and agency), professional predecessors themselves and, most of all, the files available in any agencies which have been involved. To know why a young mother is scared, hostile and abusive towards you, and to understand and emphasize (without sacrificing your own professional aims and objectives on behalf of the child) is a powerful asset during the first contact; it will greatly assist in establishing trust to enable you to begin the task of initial assessment.

Initial assessment

Many of the material facts can be quickly established, with or without mother's cooperation: numerous previous addresses, poverty, homelessness, disowned by parents, many babysitters, repetitive complaints about child being left on her own, etc. (clients nearly always cooperate in providing information about how unfair the world is to them; if one takes the trouble to listen patiently to all of this, it is easier then to suggest: 'let's now talk about everybody else's view of things'). Having established some trust, the primary objective is to explore the mother's level of awareness about the impact of the disruption, impermanency and her own absences upon her child. As in the previous case, the evidence accumulated by the midwife, health visitor, GP and social services can be used but, in this particular case, it's got to be used sparingly and sensitively. As with Rani, there are very many indicators of the damage which is being done to the child. But such indicators and professionals' observations must be referred to in such a way that they do not sound like a court verdict against the mother. The aim is to channel the mother's thinking towards her own realization of what she is unwittingly doing to the child. If she does realize, it should be acknowledged, and her potential for educating professionals about her own child should be stressed. (Many of these mothers are capable of enlightening professionals on other aspects of the abuse which the latter may not have been aware of. One mother told me that she would reach out with affection and reassurance when her child was in distress or fear, and then would suddenly withdraw, and watch the child's bewilderment quickly change to much greater fear and distress; in further exploration with the mother, 'revenge', 'control' and 'power' in an otherwise existence of bitterness, despair and powerlessness, seemed to be the motivating factors.)

The crucial component in any assessment of this type of case is the potential for mutually satisfying and fulfilling mother–child interactions. Professionals are not incapable of deceiving themselves nor of being unfair to the client in the way they observe mother and child together. In the case in question, it stated that workers were 'alarmed' on first seeing the way mother and child interacted. It may well be that the location, timing and conditions of that first sighting were far from conducive to seeing anything that wouldn't have alarmed. Professionals must also be acutely aware of the level of anxiety in the mother for the same reasons. In fact, observations and opinions about mother–child interactions, made during the *first* contact with this category of mother, should be treated with caution. (One of the problems with child abuse case conferences is that workers are not given sufficient time to make *accurate assessments* of mother–child interactions; consequently, far-reaching decisions are made on the basis of inadequate and inaccurate observation.)

It is clear from the example given that many of these young parents will have had no opportunity to learn or experience sustaining, pleasurable, positive contacts and interactions with their child. Pawan was so steeped in crisis, misery, harassment and stigma, with its consequential stress and tension – and it was long since she had known any other kind of existence – that she was incapable of responding to the child other than the way she did. Whether or not progress can be made will depend largely upon the developing relationship between the mother and professionals involved. The economic, social and cultural factors which loom so large in such cases cannot be tackled other than on the basis of trust and respect between client and worker; the problems arising from such factors have to be dealt with concurrently with continuous assessment. If the relationship *is* one of respect and trust (not necessarily agreement), if assessment is revealing new depths of self-awareness and understanding of her child's developmental needs, and if the mother is increasingly demonstrating insight into the causes and the consequences of the abuse she has been unwittingly perpetrating against the child, the prognosis must be encouraging. If, on the other hand, the mother is totally unreceptive to these efforts, and is hell-bent on sustaining a life of impermanency, disruption, chaos and recurring crises, with all the consequences for the emotional and psychological health of her child (the emotional and psychological damage clearly demonstrated in the case of Pawan), then a temporary removal of the child should be seriously considered.

Parents with mental health problems

There is no shortage of research on numerous aspects of mental illness; little has been done, however, on the extent of the impact of parents' mental illness upon children. This is surprising, if only because of the frequency of mental health problems revealed in child abuse investigations (Leeds Social Service Department, 1987) and the testimonies of those reared by parent(s) enduring long-term mental illness (e.g. Brown, 1989). The experiences of many mentally ill people are such that the emotional and psychological abuse of their children will be inevitable. The definitions we have been using are a virtual echo of the lives of many of these children. Mark's experiences (see Chapter 5) are very common.

Mental illness is often 'sustained' and 'repetitive' (i.e. recurring), as are its behavioural manifestations. Mentally ill parents, more frequently than the other categories of parent discussed, react with 'inappropriate emotional responses' to their children's emotional expressions. Often they can hardly do otherwise. Their lives are characterized by long periods of negative emotional experience (despair, fear, guilt, shame, etc.) over which they may have no control. Their illness is also likely to impair their children's psychological development (Beardslee *et al.*, 1985; Keller *et al.*, 1986; Ray, 1991). Children can hardly be expected to be able to cope with the enormity of transformation from sanity to insanity. Younger children will be unable to understand the transformation; older children may be invested with the awesome responsibility of coping with it. In either case, mental faculties, particularly intelligence development, memory and attention, can be adversely affected. So, too, may educational progress. We will look at these possibilities in more detail before seeking some guidelines for initial contact and assessment.

The complex nature of abuse by mentally ill parents

Mentally ill parents pose a more complex challenge to child care workers. Their inability to control their unwitting and unintentional abusive behaviour renders the children vulnerable to greater degrees of emotional and psychological abuse. Like many children in similar parental circumstances, Mark was being severely abused. His plea 'please look after my mammy' was a poignant indicator of the emotional, psychological and physical pain he was enduring. To repeatedly watch the breakdown of their principal carer can be a terrifying experience for small children. Workers may justifiably contemplate temporary removal. But there is a complicating factor; it revolves around the mentally ill person's concept of 'a sense of loss'. Mental health workers can recall the fear experienced by mentally ill people during the onset of their illness, the fear of losing control, losing one's contact with the world, losing the sense of reality as they plunge helplessly, yet consciously, into irrationality and the unknown. To also face the prospect of losing the last remaining yet powerful link with the world, their child, who is both a symbol and reality of the real *sane* world, is a prospect fraught with risk to parent and child alike. This in itself is sufficient to demand caution and a multidisciplinary approach to mentally ill parents who are unwittingly and unintentionally abusing their children.

Differing impacts upon differing groups of children

Attention has already been drawn to the possible different impacts of parents' mental illness upon young and old children. The differences are vast, and need further comment. A great tragedy befalling thousands of older children of mentally ill parents is increasingly being exposed (Brown, 1989): adolescents (and even younger children) often find themselves in the position of having sole responsibility for the mentally ill parent, the upkeep of the home, and the care of the remaining younger family members. It is a grossly unfair and dangerous responsibility, comprising the roles of psychiatrist (counsellor), nurse, parent (to the mentally ill parent!) and domestic. Even the most intelligent and able adolescents cannot perform these tasks. But it is becoming increasingly obvious that that is what is expected of many of them. Whose expectations are they? Mentally ill parents are not likely to expect, demand or even want their adolescent child to assume these awesome responsibilities; often their mental state is such that they are incapable of either thinking or caring about who will be responsible; the regrettable fact is that some professional mental health staff have at best ignored the welfare of children of the mentally ill and, at worst, have actually encouraged adolescent children to accept responsibility for the discharge and convalescence of their parents: 'Will your daughter or son be there when you get home . . . ?' is a common enquiry made of the patient by psychiatrist and ward staff alike, needing to alleviate themselves of their well-founded anxieties that all will not be well for the patient if the child isn't at home!

Mental health professionals and researchers generally may not yet have seen the need to focus their attention on these 'child carers' of mentally ill patients (nor have child care professionals identified them as seriously abused children), but the children themselves are taking matters into their own hands. Consequently, self-help groups are being established throughout the country, organized by young persons who have endured these impossible demands over many years. The Dolphin Project, based at the Doncaster Infirmary, is as far as I know the only initiative by mental health and therapeutic staff aimed at providing a service to the older child of mentally ill parents. Younger children, particularly infants and toddlers, are even more vulnerable to emotional and psychological abuse as a consequence of the parent's mental illness. The mentally ill parent is vulnerable too, as a consequence of the realization that when their children need them most, they can only function as emotional and mental cripples, dependent upon others for their survival. The older child, the adolescent, burdened and despairing of the impossible thankless task they have been given, at least has the advantage of understanding what is happening; they are also capable of sharing and describing their experiences with anyone who may listen. Perhaps most advantageous of all, they are able to predict some of the worst manifestations of their parent's illness, and can make preparation either to minimize it or avoid it. The younger child, in particular infants and toddlers, are not so fortunate. They cannot understand nor articulate what is happening to the parent, nor its effect upon them. They can only watch and listen, often in terror, and be totally dependent upon the remaining parent or others to protect them.

It is unlikely that child care professionals will receive too many referrals about the welfare of adolescents trying to cope with their parent's mental illness; the vast majority of referrals will be on behalf of the much younger children, visibly and audibly helpless in the face of irrational and occasionally dangerous behaviour. Despite the self-help mentioned above, adolescents are unfortunately likely to remain a largely ignored group; they are wrongly perceived to be fit and able to look after themselves, to walk away if need be. Their emotional and psychological life will not be high on the agenda during a mental health crisis precipitating hospitalization of their parent. The reality that many of them will have been subjected daily to emotional and psychological abuse over a long period of time is unlikely to enter anyone's considerations. On rare occasions, however, the adolescent will actually be the principal source of concern; for example, when the abuse has degenerated into violence; or when school staff are alarmed by the rapid deterioration in the child's performance and behaviour; above all, when the child herself begs to be removed from an insufferable and highly dangerous situation. Workers would be justified in considering alternative protective care, as much as they would be in contemplating the same for very young children. There is nothing odd or extreme about such an intervention; it should be viewed as no more drastic than the respite care social services regularly offers to tens of thousands of families.

Initial contact and assessment

Any attempt to make contact with the mentally ill parent must be based upon a thoroughly prepared strategy *formulated by the two principal agencies: child care and mental health.* This text consistently advocates multidisciplinary working on behalf of all children who are being abused emotionally and psychologically; in the case of children who are being unintentionally abused by mentally ill parents who are in need of help themselves, an approach based upon the interests of the child alone, or upon the mentally ill person alone, is doomed to failure.

Mentally ill parents are probably the least conscious of their damaging behaviour at the time it is being inflicted, i.e. during the onset or recurrence of their illness, and its more bizarre, irrational manifestations. Yet they are also probably the most guilt-ridden and frightened about the impact of the illness, whenever they have recovered sufficiently to enable them to think rationally about it. This is why the *joint* initial contact with the parent must be made with the utmost sensitivity and caution. Getting the balance of the approach right is crucial; nothing could be better calculated to further undermine what little confidence and hope the parent may have of resuming the care of the child than professionals who unwittingly speak of, or even hint at, 'the damage you are doing to your child'. Conversely, an approach which ignores the child and is blind to the fact that the child's welfare may be the paramount exacerbating factor in the mind of the parent, is likely to precipitate an even worse mental health crisis. My experience of mentally ill parents is that after the initial crisis, when they have time and the capacity to reflect, most of them are well capable of (1) realizing the impact of their illness and (2) empathizing with their children. This is one reason why one should not aim to conceal what the children have been experiencing, even less to deny it (the parent may sense any such phoney, protective strategy immediately, and may resent it bitterly or aggressively). The parent should be allowed – even encouraged – to express their feelings of fear, shame and sense of loss as a consequence of the onset of their illness. Distressing and seemingly hopeless it may be at the time, but it can later be projected as the potent source of optimism which it is: the parent who is acutely conscious of the welfare of their child, despite periodic breakdowns, still has a powerful grasp of reality, is still exhibiting a formidable loyalty and commitment.

The partner or spouse of the mentally ill parent can play a central role in maintaining a reasonable standard of care for the children. They may well be the principal person in the assessment procedure; but they may be 'principal' in more senses than one. Many of the young adolescent carers referred to are placed in the impossible 'caring' role not just because one parent is mentally ill, but very often because the other parent imposes, or suggests, or acquiesces with their adolescent accepting such a role. They should be made fully aware of the consequences for the child.

When the mentally ill person is a single parent and her children are very young, professionals will contemplate temporary alternative care. In some instances, as in the case of Mark, where the abuse may be of such a dangerous nature, temporary removal should be expedited as quickly as possible. Generally, however, the aim – in so far as their mental state may permit – is for the parent to decide for herself that her child can benefit from alternative care. Many of them will already have done so before professionals become involved. The worker should interpret that decision as indicative of the love and bond between parent and child, thus minimizing the dangerous compounded 'sense of loss' already alluded to. The parent should be given every opportunity to suggest suitable carers and accommodation. Statutory care that may enlist fostering or residential resources should be the last resort, as *familiarity* with an able, willing spouse, grandparent, aunt/uncle, close friend or neighbour, etc., may be of crucial significance to very young children who have witnessed bizarre and distressing behaviour by their parent. In the absence of this preference, workers will be aware that these children very much fall within the new Act's definition of 'children in need' (s.17(10)(b)). Local authorities have clear obligations (s.20(1)(c)) to provide alternative care and accommodation for them. Parents retain full parental responsibility (s.20(1)(c)).

Parents of children failing to thrive

'Failure-to-thrive' (FT) is a medical diagnosis which has perplexed doctors as much as it has caused anxiety in health visitors and social workers. It is commonly described as the condition in which the child is failing to grow healthily and vigorously. There are numerous physical 'organic' causes of FT, but child care professionals are primarily concerned with 'non-organic FT', indicating that the causes are not physical or organic (hereafter the abbreviation FT will refer to non-organic failure-to-thrive). The fact that this term is a medical diagnosis, whether it be organic or non-organic, is somewhat ironic, as those doctors who have focused their attention on non-organic FT are increasingly of the opinion that it *is not* a medical problem; indeed, some have gone so far as saying that a great deal of time and money is being wasted on hospitalization and laboratory tests to prove that *it is* a medical problem (Sills, 1978; Berwick *et al.*, 1982). Both of these publications advocate concentrating upon *parental* and environmental factors in seeking the causes of non-organic FT. But how, therefore, is FT related to emotional and psychological abuse? Who is abusing, and how? We need to return to our definitions, and to the relevant case history.

Failure-to-thrive as the consequence of emotional and psychological abuse

It was clear in the FT case history of two-year-old Jodie (see Chapter 5) that she was being abused emotionally and psychologically. As with many of the other cases described, the parent had no awareness of the emotionally and psychologically damaging consequences of her behaviour. There was nothing uncommon about the nature or extent of the abuse which Jodie's mother was perpetrating against her. Take the emotional abuse, for example; the repeatedly poor quality of emotional interaction between mothers and their FT infants is daily observed by many professional front-line staff, and it is supported by available literature and research (e.g. Iwaniec *et al.*, 1985; Laking, 1988; Pollitt *et al.*, 1975; Batchelor and Kerslake, 1990). It constitutes the 'sustained, repetitive, inappropriate emotional responses' of the definition. Budd (1990) speaks of the 'severe emotional deprivation' that older FT children are experiencing.

The psychological aetiology of many FT cases has long been recognized (Spitz, 1945; Widdowson, 1951). The psychological abuse inherent in this syndrome may take various forms. As in Jodie's case, the child may be perceived and treated differently (victimized) from that of the other children, and will not be able to understand why. Secondly, the child may witness her mother being victimized or humiliated by her cohabitant and/or, unintentionally, by professionals. There is, however, another far more fundamental and dangerous psychologically abusing feature: inadequate nutrition. Feeding difficulties and the lack of an effective means of coping, are nearly always the predominant features of non-organic FT cases (Sills, 1978; Iwaniec *et al.*, 1985; Batchelor and Kerslake, 1990). Medical tests may reveal such conditions as functional gastroenteritis, oesophageal reflux, chronic diarrhoea and vomiting. Medical treatment, including hospitalization, may successfully eradicate such conditions; but very often, as in the case of Jodie, children will relapse, and medical staff will concede that they often cannot find an organic cause of these illnesses. Far more important than establishing the cause is acknowledging the consequences. Inadequate nutrition, particularly in infancy, will severely damage *mental development* and, when the inadequacy has been severe in the first few months, the damage to mental development is often irreparable (Batchelor and Kerslake, 1990). The research to which these writers refer specifies 'brain damage'. That inevitably leads to damage of the mental faculties and processes discussed in Chapter 3.

Initial approach and assessment

It would be unwise to approach the parent(s) of FT children on the basis of the above introductory comments. The case of Jodie enlightens us about numerous aspects of the FT situation generally, and about the impact child care professionals in particular may have upon it. There are many lessons to be learnt, and much preparation to be made, not just in respect of the task of initial contact and assessment, but also in respect of professional perceptions and the level of self-awareness necessary to avoid self-deception and making a bad situation worse. The fact is that it is very easy for professionals to make FT cases worse, as Batchelor and Kerslake (1990), Iwaniec *et al.* (1985) and Laking (1988) have indicated. Many of these writers have identified the damaging spiral of relationships which can develop first, between the mother and a difficult-to-feed child and, secondly, between the mother and worker, e.g. health visitors, social workers, GP or nurses. The mother initially expresses concern and seeks help because the child isn't feeding properly; the professionals assess and find much fault with mother and home environment; they attempt to communicate this in the most tactful way but more often fail than succeed; the child's condition deteriorates; the professionals find they have little positive impact upon events; they become more anxious and unintentionally put more pressure upon mother; mother becomes more resentful and anxious and this adversely affects her already limited capacities for coping with the problem; eventually hospitalization is recommended; mother feels relieved but apprehensive too; the child makes a dramatic improvement in hospital and is discharged; then the child begins to deteriorate again; the professionals become more anxious and recommend a case conference in order to share their anxieties and gain a collective responsibility for assessment and action.

How best does one avoid this development? There are a number of features of Jodie's case, which, although very common in practice, have not been given the attention they deserve. First, the mother's partner is often a major contributory factor for better or worse (mainly worse!) to the overall carer/environmental context in which the child is FT. The partner is nearly always a cohabitant, and very often not the child's father. I have not yet encountered a FT case in which there is a natural father making a positive contribution to alleviating the mother of the burden of caring for the child. (This is understandable; presumably there are many cases where natural fathers do help, but such cases do not come to the notice of social services. Batchelor and Kerslake conclude from their research on FT that it is the accompanying features of 'neglect' and environmental factors which will bring FT cases to the attention of health visitors and social workers; the FT child who is cared for by loving and able middle-class parents is hardly likely to be referred to the same, nor indeed is likely to be hospitalized. Batchelor and Kerslake suggest that many FT diagnoses are in effect merely 'describing deprived children', rather than providing a credible explanation for their condition.) The most significant feature of Jodie's case is the failure of professionals to fully assess the role of the cohabitant and to engage him meaningfully this in effect constitutes an abuse of the mother.

Secondly, the health visitor and social worker find it impossible to conceal their own anxieties, and their own lack of faith in mother being able to rectify the situation. Their anxiety stems from the gravity of the problem and an acute sensitivity to the possible repercussions of some terrible calamity befalling the child. Their lack of faith in mother's coping capacities stems from (1) their awareness and observations of seemingly insurmountable problems which they rightly believe have some bearing on the FT and (2) mother's initial resentment of what they regard as helpful advice. This combination of anxiety and lack of faith is a recipe for dishonesty to the mother and self-deception between themselves (witness mother's perceptive analysis of the real reason why the health visitor and social worker want Jodie hospitalized).

Thirdly, none of the professionals involved are aware of their own contribution to the deteriorating relationship between themselves and mother. This is in fact a mirroring of what Laking (1988) refers to as the 'vicious spirals' in the relationship between mother and child:

> . . . an anxious tired mother may inadvertently communicate her tension to her baby, who, in turn, feeds poorly. This may be interpreted by the parent as criticism, which increases anxiety, and may lead to intolerance and premature cessation of feeding (p. 27).

Fourthly, none of the professionals are aware of how some of their specific actions and words make it even more difficult for mother to cope with the child, e.g. commenting on how successful others have been in coping, calling a case conference which she cannot attend, repeatedly drawing attention to hygiene factors which offend professional middle-class sensibilities far more than they can be proven to be key contributory factors to the FT.

Finally, all the professionals are so preoccupied with Jodie's FT, that they pay no heed to the remaining three children nor to mother's successful coping with them. This may have the effect of isolating Jodie further in the perceptions of mother, reinforcing her conviction that the child is exceptionally and intentionally provocative. Batchelor and Kerslake (1990) echo my own conviction expressed in the case of Rani when they write: 'Acknowledging parents as experts on their own child, who can teach the worker about the particular problems they are experiencing, is a good means of beginning to enhance the parents' sense of competence' (p. 57).

A brief profile of mothers of failure-to-thrive children

Preparation for the initial approach to FT mothers must embrace a knowledge of the available research literature, an extremely high level of communication skill and sensitivity, an appropriate style of approach, a determination to assess and engage the male partner, and self-awareness particularly about those features of the FT situation which pose the greatest challenge to each individual worker. The available literature and research on FT consistently demonstrate the hardship and misery of the principal carers, i.e. mothers. Childhood deprivation, chronic tension and anxiety, an inability to exhibit warmth and caring or to be receptive to the same, marital/relationship conflicts, permanent poverty and, not least, severe feeding problems with the child subject, are all character-istics frequently mentioned in the profiles of mothers. An awareness of these characteristics should be enough to convince workers of the vulnerability of such mothers, and just how easy it is to approach them in such a way that the inevitable outcome will be their sense of humiliation, and their lasting conviction that you represent nothing more than another of the countless hardships in their life. Consider the observation of Iwaniec *et al.* (1985: 246):

> . . . striking abnormalities in maternal feeding patterns and other caregiving performance; mothers appeared demoralized by their ineffectual attempts to feed their underweight children . . . the feeding marked by mother's anxiety, resentment and hostility, and the child's fear and resentment.

It is easy now to contemplate the impact on this type of mother and her predicament of an assessment lacking a knowledge of, and sensitivity to, the mother's plight, and carried out in an anxious, matronly-like style, characterized by tension and dishonesty.

The male cohabitant: Accepting the challenge

The presence of the male cohabitant raises questions and challenges which have to be addressed. Professional reluctance to engage and assess males has been commented on by Jordan and Packman (1978) and O'Hagan (1989). My own view is that the problem is so endemic in the child care and related professions that it constitutes institutionalized abuse of women on a massive scale. It is unwise to avoid for whatever reason a person who is likely to exercise considerable negative influence on the problem one is attempting to solve. It is grossly unfair to concentrate upon the mother, not primarily because she is the principal carer, but because she is perceived as less challenging and less threatening than the male. Finally, it is dangerous to ignore the negative influences of the cohabitant (because one hasn't a clue how to deal with them), yet to expect (and hope!) that mother can cope with them (a fatal error identified in the Tyra Henry case). The very negative role of the cohabitant in Jodie's case is typical of every single case of failure-to-thrive which I have encountered. The male cohabitant has got to be seen, heard, assessed and influenced.

Professional self-awareness in failure-to-thrive cases

In complex cases like failure-to-thrive, self-awareness assumes added significance as one attempts to plan the initial contact and assessment. Workers should be aware of how the very formidable challenges lead to a debilitating anxiety which ensures a poor quality of service at best, or unprofessional conduct at worst. How might such challenges as the poor hygiene, overcrowding, resentment and hostility, etc., affect the quality of my initial contact and assessment is the key question that the worker alone is capable of answering. But there is another related question stemming from the political/organizational context of child care: How much anxiety is being generated by an awareness of the age and vulnerability of this child? By the anxiety of my manager? By the horrible 'neglect' case I've just read about? By the letter from the very influential paediatrician at the local hospital? And what additional anxiety may be generated by your belief that the real problem (as with so many FT cases) is something akin to emotional and psychological abuse? (It should be reassuring to know that all paediatricians will not oppose this view.) It is this kind of self-exploration and making whatever preparation the answers necessitate, which will ensure a high quality of service. The action may be little more than a full and frank discussion with one's line manager, but it will be immensely valuable none the less. Together with the various other forms of preparation – knowledge of and familiarity with the profiles of the principal carers (mothers); a comprehensive grasp of the difficulties faced by the mother; a determination to engage, assess and influence the cohabitant; a consciousness of the impact of whatever style of approach you intend to adopt – all of these will greatly increase the prospects of achieving a meaningful working relationship with the family, and help avoid the pitfalls awaiting the less well-prepared.

Multidisciplinary cooperation

Considering the number of professionals involved in FT cases, multidisciplinary cooperation is important. A coherent, shared philosophy and understanding of the emotional and psychological aspects of the syndrome is necessary. The guidelines provided above are not directed to any one profession; they should be adopted by all the professionals involved. If they are not, there is the risk of one professional sabotaging the hard-earned respect of another. Nurses in wards to which children have been admitted can be an invaluable source of help and support to young mothers; they can also unwittingly and unintentionally increase the mother's anxieties by using ill-chosen words and actions (as was demonstrated in Jodie's case). GPs are often the least participative in the multidisciplinary circuit, yet they are often the most knowledgeable of the mother and her family of origin, and her current difficulties. It is imperative to inform GPs why other agencies are involved and to seek their understanding and support of the principal aims, from assessment onwards. Professionals who frequently visit the home may have difficulty in coping with exceptionally poor hygiene standards, parental resistance or an elusive unhelpful cohabitant; it's important that this is not communicated to other involved professionals as indicative of abuse in itself. Finally, there should be maximum cooperation and consistency in widening the professionals' focus beyond the diagnosis of FT. Whatever feeding difficulties exist, the child also has an emotional and psychological life. Discussing and observing the factors just mentioned, and those relationship and interactional characteristics detrimental to the child's emotional and psychological development, is equally important. Such characteristics will accelerate the process of emotional and psychological impairment caused by inadequate food intake.

Summary and conclusions

This chapter has continued with the task of demystifying emotional and psychological abuse. Numerous categories of parent/carers have been identified as frequent though unwitting and unwilling perpetrators of such abuse. These parents are not horror specimens, unique in pathology or cruelty; they are ordinary people, representative of tens of thousands of parents/carers, who, as a consequence of their misfortunes (over which many of them have no control), cannot avoid emotionally and psychologically abusing their children. We have seen, for example, how destructive in emotional and psychological terms mentally ill people can be to the children they love; they can hardly be expected either to be aware of their destructiveness when they are mentally ill, or be treated as though they are committing a criminal act. The fact is that child care professionals have always frequented the homes of psychologically and emotionally abusive parents. This chapter has concentrated on looking at four categories of such parents: (1) parents locked in vicious violent struggles preceding separation; (2) young runaway mothers, disowned by family and community alike; (3) mentally ill parents; and (4) parents of failure-to-thrive children. Each of these categories demands careful preparation for initial contact and assessment. The approach is likely to be different for each category, though the principal and pervasive aim is to reach out to the parent and avoid the many pitfalls into which one can fall and end up contributing to or intensifying the abuse the child is already suffering. Finally, as in all other cases of emotional and psychological abuse, multidisciplinary cooperation is a priority, embracing a shared philosophy, definition and understanding, and carefully planned strategy.

7

OBSERVATION, COMMUNICATION AND ASSESSMENT

Introduction

Emotional and psychological abuse is perpetrated against children regardless of their age, culture, religion or class. This chapter will concentrate on four categories of abused children, and provide guidelines and principles which are generally applicable in observing, communicating and working with them. The primacy of observation will be stressed, i.e. observation of the child, the child and carer, and child and worker. Frameworks will be provided for observing the emotional life of infants generally and failure-to-thrive infants in particular. Attention will then focus on older children (i.e. 6–9 year olds) who have endured psychological abuse unwittingly perpetrated by their alcoholic and mentally ill parents. These parents have enormous problems in their relationships within the neighbourhood, and such factors greatly exacerbate the child's misery and confusion. It is necessary to address the community aspects of the problem, for the sake of both parent and child. A detailed profile of the older emotionally abused child will be provided, concentrating on their acute difficulties in communication and integration, factors which pose major problems for the professionals in their initial contact and assessment. Finally, the psychological damage which is a direct consequence of the sexual abuse of older children will be examined, with particular attention given to the impact upon the child's moral sense and the conversion of memory to a powerful destructive force in the child's daily life.

Which children? What kind of abuse?

Emotional and psychological abuse is more common than physical and sexual abuse. The reasons are simple. First, there is always an emotionally and/or psychologically abusive consequence to physical and sexual abuse, but not vice versa; there are many cases in which the child is being abused emotionally and psychologically, but not physically or sexually. Secondly, it is much easier to abuse children when one is not aware that one is abusing them. This is often the case with emotional and psychological abuse – carers are simply not aware (there are exceptions of course). It is worth emphasizing this greater prevalency of emotional and psychological abuse before addressing the problem of approaching and serving the victims. The daunting fact is there will be some children of every age, race, culture, class, religion and nationality who have been subjected to any one of the various forms of emotional and psychological abuse, by parents, relatives, neighbours, school teachers, carers and professional child care staff. It is not within the scope of this text to examine the myriads of individual cases; what may be helpful, however, is to concentrate on those categories of abused children with whom child care workers are most familiar, and to provide guidelines and principles applicable to all cases.

Before identifying these categories, we should recall some of the deductions and conclusions made in previous chapters, particularly Chapter 3:

1 Single acts of behaviour do not constitute emotional or psychological abuse; the behaviour must be repetitive and sustained.
2 The younger the child the more easy it will be to perpetrate emotional abuse. Children in their first year are particularly vulnerable.
3 Psychological abuse of newborns and infants is difficult to ascertain because of their lack of psychological development, i.e. cognition, perception, intelligence, memory, recognition and attention.
4 Research indicates that emotional abuse is a prominent characteristic in cases of non-organic failure-to-thrive infants.
5 Psychological abuse is very common when the principal carer is mentally ill or an alcoholic.
6 Adolescent children who have experienced normal and healthy emotional and psychological development may be more resistant and less damaged by current emotional and psychological abuse.
7 Psychological abuse is inherent in many forms of sexual abuse, particularly father–daughter incest.

The categories of children upon which this chapter will now concentrate are: (a) infants generally and failure-to-thrive infants in particular; (b) children of alcoholic and mentally ill parents; (c) emotionally abused older children; and (d) older children who have been sexually abused by their father. (The term 'older' refers to children between the ages of six and nine.) The first task in respect of all these children is systematic observation.

The primacy of observation

Child care staff need no reminding of the importance of observation. But in cases of suspected emotional and psychological abuse, it is of such crucial significance that its primacy and basis for all subsequent action has to be spelt out in some detail.

First, from the child's point of view, it may be very difficult to let professionals know what is happening. This is a major problem in sexual abuse cases, and professionals have devoted a good deal of effort learning how to enable children to indicate or expose sexual abuse. They also have the advantage of quickly putting their suspicions to the test through increasingly more reliable medical examination. Consider how infinitely more difficult it is to enable children, particularly those who are very young to indicate or expose emotional or psychological abuse? The most sophisticated, educated and intelligent young child will have great difficulty. And there is no quick test available if one does suspect such abuse. *The emotionally and psychologically abused child is more dependent upon professional observation than any other category of abused child.*

Secondly, there is a parallel between the meaning of 'observation' and the core of the definition of emotional and psychological abuse; just as that kind of abusive behaviour must be repetitive and sustained, so too must the observations of all professionals involved in the case. This is more problematic than it sounds, and possibly painful too; it necessitates many contacts with the child and the principal carer over a considerable period of time; it may necessitate unpleasant detailed observations of how the carer treats the child, i.e. speaks to her, lifts her, feeds her, clothes her, or ignores her, and the immediate and longer-term effects. Initially, the professional must in effect be an objective researcher, exercising self-control, and ensuring that the unpleasantness of the observation does not minimize the capacity to record it accurately, nor compel one to intervene precipitantly. If observation is a shared exercise between agencies, the less painful and the more objective it will be.

Observing failure-to-thrive infants

There are differing levels of observation. Even the most basic level may reveal substantive material requiring further exploration and confirmation. Carroll and Williams (1988) give examples of this when they write: 'the effects of . . . emotional abuse are so damaging that they are often clearly visible in such behaviour as clinging or withdrawal, hyperactivity, broken sleep patterns, delayed speech and poor appetite . . .' (p. 20). When dealing with specific categories of children, however (e.g. failure-to-thrive), systematic and detailed observations are required, as in Iwaniec *et al.* (1986). Under the heading of physical description, they observed: 'wasted body, thin arms and legs, large stomach, red cold and wet hands and feet, thin wispy dull, and sometimes falling hair, dark circles around the eyes'. Under the heading 'psychological description', they observed the following: 'sadness, expressionless face, general lethargy, withdrawal, detachment, depression, bursting into tears, frequently whining, minimal or no smiling, diminished vocalization, staring blankly at people or objects, lack of cuddliness, unresponsiveness, lack of proper stranger anxiety . . .' (p. 246). It should be stressed that none of these observations, either separately or collectively, suggest that a child is being emotionally or psychologically abused; they merely reflect upon the professional approach and rigour of the observers.

The most sophisticated observations, however, do suggest some link between FT and emotional abuse; these were made by Abramson (1991) in his research into facial expressivity of twelve FT subjects, aged between six and 25 months (there was a matching control group of twelve healthy infants). The research was based upon Tomkins's (1962) theory of affect and Darwin's original observations on facial expressivity (1872). Abramson (1991) writes:

> Tomkins has argued that the emotions comprise the primary motivational system of the personality. *Further, the face is the primary site of that motivation for self and other; it is, if you will, our interface with the world. For infants, these facial expressions are their language* . . . and the felt experience of the emotions associated with them give impetus and direction to behaviour (p. 162, my emphasis).

Abramson and his research team video-recorded no less than 3196 facial movements as part of 1917 facial emotional expressions. The emotions were interest, joy, surprise, sadness, anger, disgust, contempt, fear and distress. The details of these observations are paralleled by the variety and range of emotional expressivity revealed, and by the significance of the researchers' conclusions. For example, contrary to much anecdotal evidence, there was no significant difference in the sum total of facial emotional expressivity between the FT and the control group of children. Abramson draws attention to the fact that FT children are often observed as 'listless' or as having 'flat affect' (meaning very little emotional expression). He implies that many of these observations may be inaccurate, as the observer, when pressed, will speak of the same children having 'sad' or 'wary' expressions, the point being that the child is expressing negative emotion rather than no emotion at all. The major finding in Abramson's research was that the emotional expressions and experiences of FT children were predominantly negative, i.e. fear, sadness, anger, distress, contempt and disgust. But there is a crucial distinction to be made:

> A baby who truly is listless and has flat affect gives virtually no cues to a potential caregiver concerning its needs and what it is feeling. Yet the infant who is constantly sad or wary continues to provide a caregiver with some information concerning its internal state, and still can elicit an adaptive response from an adult. Theoretically, these latter infants would be less at risk than the former.

(Practitioners may say it's this constant expression of negative emotion which heightens the risk of parents injuring the child). Abramson continues:

> The infant who displays more fear or sadness presumably feels more of these emotions. Although the high levels of negative affect suggest that life is not very pleasant for these babies, at least the affective mechanisms which have evolved to produce certain patterns of arousal, stimulation, and feedback, are intact and functioning. Such stimulation may provide internal signals which help infants organise their behaviour and gain some relief by means of self-comforting (p. 174).

(FT infants were seen to engage in a much higher level of self-comforting.)

This research questions many of the assumptions made on the basis of 'superficial' observation. Although the group of children being researched represent a specific, highly characterized category of at-risk children, the findings are significant for child care professionals observing and assessing the emotional development of any infant. Abramson describes an eighteen-month-old FT child who smiled more often than any other child (including those in the control group); careful study of the video replay, however, revealed that her smile was not elicited by pleasurable things, but, rather, each time she oriented towards another person. Furthermore, the researchers soon realized her smile was created by an unusual facial musculature more commonly associated with a sad or weary brow. Hers was not a genuine smile, more a means of adapting to the persons and stimulation she was encountering, suggestive of a perception that these were hostile or threatening.

Table 7.1 Emotional interactions between carer and child

Emotion felt and/or expressed by infant	Examples of appropriate emotional responses of carer	Examples of inappropriate emotional and other kinds of response of carer
Interest	Interest/curiosity, praise, encouragement	Disinterest, annoyance, anger, removal of source of interest
Joy and laughter	Joy, pride, laughter, enthusiasm in sharing	Indifference, annoyance, anger, threatening (SHUT UP!)
Distress	Comforting (verbally and physically)	Ignoring, rejecting, indifference, mocking
Anger	Disapproval, disappointment, reassurance	Greater anger, submission, threat or violence
Fear	Comforting/reassuring, explaining/familiarizing, praising (the fear may well be justified and necessary)	Anger, irritation, mockery, isolating, threatening or violence

Infant-carer(s) interactions

Observation of the infant is unlikely in the absence of the principal carer. Excellent though Abramson's research is, it says virtually nothing about the presence of the infant's carers. For child care workers, this is the crucial factor: What was the carer doing (if anything) to elicit the emotional expressivity of her child? Or, what was his/her emotional response to the child's emotional expressivity caused by some stimulus other than herself? Because the carer's emotional responses to the child's emotional expressivity is the core issue for the prospect of emotional development, workers must be particularly careful about the recording of their observations. Just as we have familiarized ourselves with emotions the infant may feel and express, so too must we familiarize ourselves with the range of possible emotional responses by the carer – both appropriate and inappropriate responses – to those common emotional expressions of infants (see Table 7.1).

The principal task is establishing whether or not these healthy or unhealthy emotional interactions are entrenched patterns of communication, or isolated untypical incidents. If they are habitual and entrenched, there may well be sound historical reasons. Being aware of the atmosphere and prevailing moods is important, as is the ability to describe it convincingly. Our second framework can then consist of direct questions on each of these contextual matters. They can only be answered on the basis of (a) numerous visits and opportunities to observe, (b) good liaison and sharing of observations with the other professionals involved, (c) a relationship of trust and mutual understanding between worker and family (nothing could be more futile nor unjust than a situation in which there is mutual antipathy between worker and family; the worker's visit increases anxiety and anger, and repeatedly provokes those type of emotional interactions which may convince the worker that the child is being emotionally abused: see the case of Jodie, Chapter 5; see also FT parents, Chapter 6).

Questions on the wider context of infant–carer interactions

1 Are the emotional interactions between the carer and infant repetitive and sustained, or are they inconsistent, without pattern or form? Have they been predictable, or are there factors/conditions which make them unpredictable, e.g. mental health problems, alcoholism, cohabitant?

2 If you are repeatedly observing inappropriate emotional responses, can you discern any consistency in time, location, original stimulus for the unhealthy emotional interactions? You and your colleagues from other agencies may observe that the carer is harsh in handling the infant and repeatedly responds inappropriately at a particular time of the day, before or after a daily habitual incident, action or event; or, more seriously, you may observe that the carer always responds emotionally inappropriately; or, you may observe that it is the presence and behaviour of another (e.g. cohabitant) which consistently precedes inappropriate emotional responses to the infant.

3 What has been the prevailing mood and/or atmosphere surrounding the infant–carer interactions which you have repeatedly observed? Is it one of tension, violence, distress, anger or indifference, or is it more often hustle and bustle, intermittent banter and humour?

4 Is there chronic poverty in the home? Is there persistent pressure from other agencies about other matters (e.g. education: non-school attendance; police: investigating crime, perceived and felt as harassment)? Are there recurring threats from debt collectors?

5 What can the carer(s) recall of the patterns of communication in their own families of origin? Are the current emotional interactions merely the continuation of the cycle? (The method and language of such an exploration will determine how far one may go; noticing and commenting upon the carer's predominant emotion in a non-critical way is always a good starting point for exploring carers' childhoods.)

Observation of interactions during feeding of failure-to-thrive infants

Difficulty in feeding is the principal cause of non-organic failure-to-thrive (Batchelor and Kerslake, 1990). The nature of the interactions which take place during feeding may be such as to constitute either emotional or psychological abuse. The following questions will enable workers to explore that possibility as well as making an important contribution to assessment.

1 Is there consistency in which carer feeds the child, mealtimes, location, seating? Is the seating age-appropriate? Does the child look and feel comfortable? Is the child 'trapped', i.e. held tightly in the arm, or left dangerously reaching up to the high table for each spoonful? Are mealtimes rushed, in an anxious, strife-laden atmosphere?
2 Which meals cause the greatest difficulty for the child, solids or liquids? Breakfast, lunch or tea? Which is most difficult for the carer?
3 How does the carer feel as she approaches the task of feeding? How does she feel halfway through feeding, at the end of feeding?
4 How do you think the child feels at each of these times above?
5 How would you describe the actions of the carer during feeding: gentle/ rough, careful/careless, patient/impatient, enjoyable/unpleasant, re- laxing/anxiety-provoking, confident/fearful? Give a detailed descrip- tive account of the action which warrants any of these terms?
6 What emotions have you observed in the child during feeding? Does she turn away and spit her food out? Does she refuse to open her mouth? Is she sick soon after? Does she vomit? Diarrhoea? How does the carer react?
7 What domestic/marital/financial or other factors have you observed as having a major impact upon the quality of feeding, for better or worse? Is the child a witness to domestic strife generally, and mother battering in particular?
8 What impact, good or bad, do you as the visiting professional have upon the quality of feeding?

Worker–infant interactions

The worker should take ever opportunity to interact with the child, verbally and physically. If such an opportunity does not easily arise, the worker should facilitate it. This may pose practical problems and ethical considerations: the infant may be asleep; the parent may resent anyone, particularly a professional person, from handling their child; the worker may feel that they have no right to seek to communicate physically or merely to hold the child; the child herself may have an aversion to anyone, or anyone other than the principal carer touching her; in the case of the older infant (12–18 months), some workers may have strong convictions about the risk of sexual abuse in later years resulting from too much physical contact with strangers earlier. All these genuine resistances should be seriously considered and respected; but the interactions between a worker and the infant are so fundamentally a part of the assessment process (Carroll and Williams, 1988) that workers and managers must together overcome them. If a referred infant is more often asleep, the worker is going to have to find out when she is more often awake, and visit then; sleeping infants may be a source of interest to some, they are hardly likely to enlighten one seeking indications of the infant's emotional life! If a parent resents someone touching their infant, the worker must patiently establish a relationship whereby s/he will be made an exception. Acknowledgement and praise of a parent's resentment of anyone touching her child can be a useful beginning to achieving such a relationship. In the meantime, the worker can explore eye-to-eye contact, and the impact of their own movements upon the infant and, in particular, the impact of their varying speech. Always, the worker should be comparing/contrasting these impacts with those made by the carer(s); always, they should display a certain deference to parents in respect of any request to advance beyond whatever level of interaction has been achieved. Part of the difficulty may be the entrenched customs and beliefs of professionals, e.g. the midwife or health visitor is the one who 'touches' babies, the social worker is the one who talks to their parents. These customs and beliefs are unhelpful. Health visitors, midwives and doctors will as always remain primarily responsible for assessing the *physical* health of infants; social workers, because of their family and community-oriented responsibilities, have the primary statutory responsibility for assessing emotional development and/or emotional abuse. Frequent visits and observations of an infant without any attempt to make physical contact, to play with, touch, talk and listen to the child, can only minimize the quality of assessment.

The recent exposure of child sexual abuse has had disastrous consequences on some professionals' perceptions of 'touching'. An unhelpful legacy remains whereby parents in general and fathers in particular perceive danger more than benefit in touching; whereby social workers' traditional reluctance to handle babies has intensified, and infants and toddlers, particularly those who have experienced the horrors of sexual abuse, are pounced upon whenever they reach out to the nearest adult. I know of one large authority's training course for foster parents, which vigorously discouraged touching between the sexually abused child and the foster parents given the task of caring for them! Carroll and Williams (1988) have no doubt about the necessity of professionals physically engaging the child in the interests of assessment. While acutely aware of a parent's feelings and rights, Carroll and Williams nevertheless stress:

the social worker needs to show a child, for example, he is allowed to climb on her knee . . . much of our communication involves touch . . . reassuring touch, stimulating touch, controlling touch . . . repetitiveness of play will help . . . singing the same rhyme together . . . children play on the floor, and the social worker needs to be with the child, mentally and physically . . . children need to be seen frequently, as often as two or three times a week . . . (pp. 20–22).

Regrettably, this article was published before the crisis of child sexual abuse erupted; it could well do with a reprint!

Psychological abuse: The older child

Some may think it easier to assess emotional and psychological abuse of older children because cognitive development enables them to conveniently tell us what's happening to them! Also, their emotional expression (or lack of it) is visibly and audibly more pronounced. There are, however, differing stages at which contact with the child will be made, and many complex social and multidisciplinary factors that can make communicating and working with such children more hazardous than convenient. Patience, persistence, sensitivity and tolerance are required, plus the relevant theoretical knowledge, skills and technique. Before exploring effective agency responses, let us be reminded of the nature and consequences of the abuse which many older children are enduring.

Mark and Tony (see Chapter 5) are typical of children enduring psychological abuse. One is the child of a mentally ill parent and the other the child of an alcoholic parent. The psychological abuse in Mark's case is manifest in his mother's irrational, unpredictable, often violent outbursts, and her disintegration into helplessness and self-pity. The psychological consequences are: an underlying anxiety and fear that his mother will behave like this again; a lack of confidence in shaping and planning his own destiny; his reluctance to take any initiative or believe that his situation might improve; a chronic lack of attentiveness in school (and non-attendance); a distorted perception of the world with a consequential developing neurosis, and undermining of moral development. The psychological abuse in Tony's case is manifest in similar ways: he too has no control over his own destiny; his mother is frequently paralytic; she sabotages his relationships with the outside world, creating enormous stigma, and making him an object of pity; in school, his attentiveness and performance are severely limited; so too is meaningful social contact and integration; he has a pervasive dread of his mother humiliating him again in the presence of his peers, and he resorts to lies and other potentially immoral means of avoiding it. A famous American alcohol and drug treatment centre (Lincoln General Hospital, Nebraska) describes the plight like this:

> Where other children live with encouragement, praise, acceptance, approval, fairness and honesty, the child of an alcoholic lives with hostility, criticism, fear, jealously and self-pity. Where other children live with friendliness and learn that the world is a nice place to live in, the child from the alcoholic home lives with hostility and believes fighting is the way to relate (1988, p. 5).

The initial 'crisis' response

Either of these cases could be referred in various ways. The referral is most commonly made by a neighbour. Once again, she has witnessed 'this poor child' being subjected to 'madness' or 'badness', and she thinks it's deplorable that nobody's doing anything about it. The neighbours will know precisely what to do about it: remove the child! Friends, enemies, relatives and police will be enlisted to drive home the point. A clear distinction should be made here between the challenges of initial response and the later challenges posed by the task of a comprehensive assessment. Yet the two sets of challenges are linked, inherent components of a process in which the initial response may be crucial in determining the difficulty and quality of the comprehensive assessment which must follow later. These referrals constitute a major crisis for child, parent, neighbours and professionals alike, and some understanding of crisis theory, crisis processes and community crisis intervention techniques are imperative (see Bott, 1971; Morrice, 1976; O'Hagan, 1986, 1991). It is particularly necessary to deal effectively with the neighbourhood and community aspects of these crises before focusing upon the child. The neighbours have got to be thanked for making the referral, and their trust gained by demonstrating that something really is going to be done. Otherwise, their influence on the situation generally and *upon the psychological state of the child in particular will remain potentially destructive* (see below).

What we are primarily concerned about, however, is the way that some of the characteristics and processes of such crises and inappropriate interventions can become a mere extension, or worse, an intensification, of the psychological abuse the child has already suffered. These referrals give professionals an invaluable opportunity (should they be able to respond immediately) to witness a typical phase of emotional and psychological abuse as it is actually being perpetrated and, more importantly, to witness how the child responds and the impact upon him. (I realize this may sound morbid and obscene, but it is *invaluable* in the sense of enabling the professional to give testimony with confidence and conviction in later consultations with the child, parent, colleagues and, should it be necessary, magistrates.)

The abuse may be so obvious, and the immediate parental condition so hopeless, that professionals may initially contemplate a massive intervention, such as temporary removal. This indeed may be in accord with the welfare principle of the Children Act, more specifically those sections which repeatedly declare the obligation to protect the child from significant harm. But removal is only likely to be seriously contemplated if one believes the child is also in imminent danger of physical attack. Care must be taken in assessing whether or not the child really is in danger of attack from a parent, or whether or not it is the perceived threat of intervention which looks like provoking the mother's attack upon the professional rather than the child! The child's own views and feeling about this matter should be sought; these may differ substantially from those within a professional perspective.

There is one final matter that may be of significance in assessment during these common types of crises. It's not unusual to find appalling standards of hygiene: carpets and furniture heavily stained; piles of unwashed clothes stretching towards the ceiling; dishes that haven't been washed for days; the grass touching the window sills, dog dirt everywhere; and a pervasive stench wherever one might be in the home. Many types of mental illness and alcoholism, and the isolation endured by the victims, are not exactly conducive to maintaining an acceptable level of hygiene standards. Psychological abuse is often inextricably linked with the material world around the child – indeed, may be dependent upon it for some of its effect. Objects, possessions, shapes and design, movements, sight, sound and smell, may become fused, in the child's perception, with the more direct psychologically abusive behaviour. How the drunken parent staggers up the garden path, stumbles between the table and couch, throws the coat on the mounting unwashed pile, collapses into the favoured armchair, and then proceeds with a half hour's verbal garbage, punctuated by burping and farting – all this may be as psychologically detrimental to the child as, for example, the unreliability of the parent, the frights he endures in repeatedly seeing the parent about to fall, set the house on fire, accidentally kill him/herself with a knife, or daily threatening to attack those 'bastard' neighbours who want the parent evicted and the child removed.

Precisely the same point can be made about the material world of the child psychologically abused by the mentally ill parent, or any other parent for that matter. It is not just significant in attempting to assess the child's experiences, but the worker must also realize that such factors as hygiene are crucially significant in the perceptions of neighbours, and that it is precisely this point – what the neighbours, 'the parents of my street friends', think, say and do (or threaten to do) – which bears most heavily on the mind of the child.

Caring for parents: Establishing good relationships with the child

Despite the cruel nature of the psychological abuse being unwittingly perpetrated against these children, it is abundantly clear that both of them have powerful feelings of loyalty towards their mothers. Arising from this loyalty is a debilitating guilt: first, the child feels guilty because he cannot protect his mother from the consequences of her own actions; secondly, he may also feel guilty because – as is clearly the case with Mark – he is made to feel responsible for his mother's bizarre behaviour; and, thirdly, he is most likely to feel guilty in sensing, even witnessing, the hostility of neighbours towards his mother. Any approach to these children should avoid intensifying their sense of guilt. It would be quite simple to do so by unwittingly stressing how bizarre or unfair mother's behaviour has been, or by marginalizing mother and her influence by focusing entirely upon the child, or by being unduly influenced by the powerful collective voice of a disgusted and angry neighbourhood. Any such approach would likely engender a sense of betrayal in the child, thereby intensifying the guilt. The fact is that these mothers remain immensely powerful figures in the lives and perceptions of their children, for good as well as ill.

Irrespective of how severe the alcoholic or mental illness condition is, each child will be conscious of the times when their mothers were neither paralytic nor mentally ill; they will cling onto a hope that it can always be like that. As Mark himself poignantly demonstrated, such children will be greatly relieved in the knowledge that their parents are going to be helped (rather than condemned), so that that hope of normality can be realized. Here is where tolerance and patience may be sorely tested. The social worker responding to the referral may have to endure torrents of threats and/or abuse from either parent. Drunken parents in particular are difficult to deal with, and, generally speaking, should be left until they sober up. It is sometimes difficult to avoid being harsh and dismissive of such parents. One should be aware of the consequence upon a child who may witness it. The initial approach to the child, therefore, has to be based upon a demonstrable concern for mother, reassuring the child that her needs, her problems (not the least of which is her alienation within the neighbourhood, in itself an enormous source of misery for the child), will be addressed. These can only be addressed by frequent returns to the family home, consultation and negotiation with neighbours and relevant agencies, and sincerity; anything less is a betrayal of the child, and a further contribution to the abuse they've already endured. Furthermore, if the assessment which is to follow concludes that protection from long-term psychological damage can only be achieved by removal, such drastic steps will be less traumatic to a child who has witnessed strenuous efforts made on his mother's behalf.

Referrals from school

Another common source of referral on these types of abused children is the school teacher. Here, happily, there is no community crisis to deal with, and the process of professional assessment has already begun (how agencies respond may determine whether or not a community crisis will develop). There is no professional better placed to observe the consequences of psychological abuse than classroom teachers. Work performance, levels of concentration and attentiveness, perception (as manifest through written work, art and play), language, and changing relationships within peer groups – all these may be repeatedly observed and monitored over a sufficiently long enough period to convince teaching staff that there is a serious problem necessitating referral to a child care agency. A major ethical problem then arises: does the child care professional respond by visiting the school and interviewing the child without the parent knowing? My own view is that they should not, that the parent should be contacted (which will in itself be an important part of the assessment process) and told of the school's concern, and be invited to accompany the worker to the school. If the parent is enduring a period of mental instability or is blind drunk, then the worker may justifiably consider visiting the school alone, or in the company of a sympathetic relative. Should the parent accompany the worker, the child should be well-prepared by teaching staff. The child may feel relieved on the one hand that someone is taking an interest, but, on the other, he may be fearful, anticipating some terrible calamity if his mother wrongly believes that he has betrayed her to the authorities. All these possibilities need to be considered jointly by teaching and child care staff, and contingency plans made.

Engaging the psychologically abused child

A sufficient profile of the psychologically abused child and his family and social context has now been drawn to indicate that communication and relationship building is not going to be easy; it is, however, the social and family context, and not the child, which compels one to embark upon the communicative task with caution. Once again, patience, resilience and dogged persistence will prove beneficial. It actually isn't all that important if one does not succeed in communicating with the child on initial contact; the evidence of impairment of psychological development is available elsewhere, and difficulties or setbacks in communicating and relationship building should not impede progress on making a comprehensive assessment. This should be made on as expansive a base as possible, involving numerous agencies. Previous records, for example, in social services offices and GP clinics, may be important in establishing the origins and severity of the parent's difficulties; these may be entirely compatible with school records which can pinpoint accelerated deterioration in the child's performance and behaviour. The local police station in particular, the 'patch bobby' is most likely to know of an alcoholic or mentally ill parent in his patch, and will have relevant information about the social and community aspects of the problem. Psychiatric, school psychological and voluntary services may also be involved; if so, they have to be contacted and given the opportunity of contributing to the assessment process.

This accumulation of information and the time it has taken actually makes the renewed task of communicating with the child easier. The crisis (and possibly the trauma) of initial contact and concerns by various professionals has now passed; the child has seen for himself that no undue pressure has been applied, no phoney exaggerated friendliness attempted, no insensitive parent-bashing visits made. Within this context, it will be easier to approach the child, and eventually to converse about the painful phases of abuse in their lives. Psychologically abused older children, unlike those who have been persistently emotionally abused, do not normally have inherent difficulty in communicating. Their communicative faculties are not necessarily impaired as a consequence of the psychological abuse described in Tony and Mark's case. Remember the definition, and the principal consequence of such abuse: 'undermining the child's attempt to understand the world around him; confusing him and frightening him.'

In these circumstances, as with the cases of Tony and Mark, the psychologically abused child cries out for the adult to communicate with him, to rescue him, and to demonstrate a world that will make sense to him. The professional need only decide on the appropriate time. Provided they have taken the necessary precautions in avoiding action and words which exacerbate the burden and miseries of the child's life (in other words, dealt effectively with parental and community context of the abuse), then communication and relationship building will be welcomed by the child. More importantly, it can lead to the child's courageous expression of ultimate need, namely, that his life has become so miserable in the care of his parent that he wishes to be removed. I can recall a nine-year-old psychologically abused child of a single alcoholic father; my colleague's consistent compassion and patience with the father and her highly sensitive and patient work with the child eventually led to the child's own request (in the presence of his father) to be removed. As Lee (1991) points out, the psychologically abused child is well capable of 'astonishingly powerful verbal communications at times' (p. 25).

Emotional abuse: The older child

Exploration of emotional development and the definition of emotional abuse suggests the probability of important characteristics in the older emotionally abused child.

1 The child's emotional life is dominated by *negative emotion*, or the *repression* of all emotion.
2 *Difficulty in communicating, relating and integrating*. Emotion is crucially significant in facilitating communication, particularly positive emotions; the emotionally abused child who has learnt to adapt to or survive the abuse by expressing as little emotion as possible, or by expressing negative emotion predominantly , will have severe communication difficulties. These will cause major problems in relationship building and social integration.
3 *Bizarre behaviour*. The older emotionally abused child gains a larger repertoire of tactics for avoiding emotional contact and emotional expression. These tactics are often perceived by the onlooker as bizarre. They include the appearance of deadness, frozen watchfulness, or the other extreme of violent recoil from emotion-laden words or actions, particularly those which are warm and friendly.
4 *Physical abuse*. It is highly likely that the emotionally abused child will also have endured physical abuse. This is usually admitted by the carer. Ironically, the reason often given for the physical abuse is that the child persistently 'ignores' the carer; this usually means the child justs stares at the carer screaming at her; the carer does not realise that the child may be incapable of the response which is required. The 'ignoring' is anything but; it is merely the child's defensive/avoidance posture.

Characteristics like these make life extremely difficult for the inexperienced worker. The unhappiness of the child is immediately apparent, and makes one want to attempt to engage her as quickly as possible. Some calm reflection on such characteristics, however, will advise against haste, and provide some pointers as to initial approach and contact. As with the psychologically abused child, there are numerous channels along which the professional will encounter the older emotionally abused child. Differing strategies are needed.

Referrals are most commonly made by schools, and, as point (4) above suggests, by the carers themselves. But they may also be made by neighbours, friends, relatives or agencies. Carers are typically unaware of emotional abuse and even less aware of the reality that they may be perpetrating it. While this may present some difficulty, it often has the advantage that the carers are not fearful about seeking help from child care agencies. They often welcome professional help for what they see as a problem definitely not of their making. Assessment of the emotionally abused child will be based upon (1) frequent visits and observations of the child and carer(s) together, (2) unobtrusive observations of the child, particularly in the school setting, (3) observations of and interactions with the child alone and (4) consultation and liaison with all care agencies who have been involved with the child or family.

Once again, classroom teachers are in a uniquely privileged position to contribute to the assessment process. Over a long period of time each day, they can observe the type and limitations of emotional expressivity of the child; how limited is the child's emotional range? What/when are the most conspicuous inappropriate emotional responses? (e.g. how does the child respond to banter or bullying, to praise or criticism?). The school referral about the emotionally abused child does not imply that the child's work has deteriorated; remember, emotional abuse may, but does not *necessarily*, adversely affect the functioning of mental processes upon which intellectual performance largely depends; indeed, school life and the intellectual stimulation it provides (as opposed to the abusive and unavoidable emotional life at home) is sometimes regarded as a haven by the emotionally abused child, and their work performance does not deteriorate. Careful scrutiny of school records and listening to the observations of the teacher will clarify whether or not one is dealing solely with emotional abuse.

Observing emotional interactions between carer(s) and child

Frequent visits to the home of the emotionally abused child is a necessary requirement for assessment. A similar framework as was used in assessing emotionally abused infants may be useful (see p. 105). But there will be a marked difference in the level of emotional expression by the older child. Persistent inappropriate emotional responses by the carer(s) will have rendered the child incapable of experiencing positive emotion. One should not, however, interpret the lack of visible and audible emotional expression as 'an emotional-less child'. As the research of Abramson demonstrates, it is more likely that the child is experiencing and expressing the less visible and less audible negative emotion. Whether the emotional expression is negative or non-existent, the child is likely to to be viewed by the carer more as a provocation than a subject of concern. Their way of coping with the child is, ironically, an intensification of the inappropriate emotional responses which have created the problem in the first instance. It is extremely unpleasant to witness the intensifying cycles of emotional abuse which these responses constitute;

but little understanding of the problem can be gained without such observations. (It is also ironical that parents will restrain themselves from even the most minor physical chastisement in the worker's presence, but will feel no such restraint in emotionally abusive behaviour.) Particular attention should be given to any part played in the cycle by family members other than the principal carer. How precisely they become involved should be noted (the more involvement the more complex and difficult the case).

Material factors like hygiene, possessions, furniture, etc., may be as significant as they were in the case of the psychologically abused child: the bedroom door with the bolt on the outside; the discarded drawings which the child brought home from school and nobody looked at; the filthy urinated bedsheets which the carer does not change because the child 'refuses' to speak; the empty cage where once the white mice (that the parents could not stand) roamed – the parents eventually drowned the mice – all these possibilities have to be noted carefully and preliminary assessment made of their meaning for the child. They may well represent the most palpable manifestation of the emotional abuse, their very existence sustaining that abuse in the heart and mind of the child.

Finally, workers should seek out any other perceptions which the carers may have of the child, and explore the carers' potential for understanding the nature of emotional abuse and whether or not they can respond to it differently. This, too, will necessitate a tactful but comprehensive investigation about the carers' own upbringings, in particular seeking to establish whether or not the existing emotional abuse is merely an extension of patterns of communication established over generations. If this is the case, the carers' opinion about the influence of that past upon the way they respond to their own children will be crucial. There is some guidance about questions to be asked, in the Department of Health's *Protecting Children* (1988, pp. 50–2); but one needs to be selective, however, as many of the 98 questions are not relevant to the task now being pursued.

Initial approach and engagement with the emotionally abused older child

There should be little problem in gaining parents' approval for seeing the child without them attending; there will be even less resistance on the part of the child. During initial contacts, the child may appear frozen, silent, withdrawn, remote; or she may recoil from any attempt made to reach out to her; or babble to herself about something only she knows and understands; or engage in some ritualistic or neurotic behaviour, apparently oblivious to the world around her. These may all be avoidance tactics which the child has cultivated, keeping at bay the emotional contact which she has come to dread. Any attempt to impose oneself upon the child, particularly through friendly humorous conversation, will only intensify her tactics. The child who adopts tactics like these in order to avoid emotional contact is seriously emotionally abused. The worker who witnesses a child behaving like this is almost certain to have witnessed inappropriate emotional responses by the carer. The strategy of intervention required is two-pronged: regular therapeutic work with the child by expert play therapists and supportive and intensive counselling of the carer. Initially, these must be separate strategies: even the most experienced and skilled counsellor/family therapist would not be able to avoid considerable risk to the already damaged child by immediately engaging carers and child together. Such work can be attempted when the therapeutic work with the child has made significant progress.

The sexually abused child: Emotional and psychological consequences

Here is a simple observation about the case of Caroline, the sexually abused child encountered in Chapter 5. The parents are professional people, intelligent, educated. The abusing father is a sophisticated criminal, using his professional acumen and experience gained in caring for children as a means of ensnaring his own child. The more sophisticated the method of ensnaring a child for the purpose of sexually abusing her, then the more effective will be the abuse in 'confusing and frightening' the child, and in 'undermining the child's attempt to understand the world around her' (i.e. psychological abuse; also, the impact upon the child's creative and developmental potential of such faculties as intelligence, memory, perception, attention and moral sense will be adverse). Another way of putting this is: the more successful the perpetrator is in playing out two entirely opposite roles, i.e. that of a loving father and evil perpetrator, the more difficult it will be for the child to cope. Child protection workers encounter enormous variation in the levels of sophistication and 'success' by which abusers can sustain the abuse. The least intelligent with their less sophisticated tactics are more likely to be exposed. The more intelligent and cunning devote countless hours formulating strategies which ensure they will not be exposed. The former pose less risk to the child; their attempt to abuse may be so blatant and clumsy that the child herself can see it coming, and may feel able to challenge it; certainly at least, there is less chance of the child being confused by such a perpetrator – he is evil and wicked, and that's that! The latter, like Caroline's father, will cause the maximum confusion in the child's mind. Their cunning ensures not only the unlikelihood of them being exposed but also intensification of the child's fear, distress and helplessness.

There are numerous research studies and theoretical formulations now available to indicate the serious short- and long-term effects of sexual abuse (e.g. Wyatt and Powell, 1988; Gomes-Schartz *et al.*, 1990). Finkelhor *et al.* (1988) conceptualize the effects in terms of 'traumatic sexualization', 'betrayal', 'stigmatization', and 'powerlessness'. Furniss (1991) concentrates upon the sophisticated cunning and deception of the abuser. The abuser creates three contextual levels upon which to pursue his desires in a way in which the experience of the sexual abuse by the child will be 'undone' and 'negated'.

First (precisely as Caroline's father did), he creates a context in which it's inconceivable to the child that he intends to abuse her; this may be facilitated by goodies like chocolates, banter or play; or, more mysteriously, by silence, without eye contact, or in a darkened room with the curtains drawn (the latter initially creates the impression that father may be indulging in some new game; but there is not the slightest hint of harm). The various sexual acts may then begin:

> The physical sensations of the abuse and the interactional context created . . . leads to a conflicting, and contradictory physiological perceptual and emotional double experience . . .
>
> The intense skin contact and the body stimulation constitute the sexual aspect of sexual abuse. The confusing sensory experience of the sexual act happens in a context in which the abuser tries to deny that the abuse takes place at all. The sexual nature of sexual abuse is meant to be split off and undone by the abuser through minimizing the input of other sensory modes which negate the ongoing abuse. This is achieved through silence, darkness, ritualized physical contact, avoidance of eye contact, and many ritualized aspects of the interaction. The undoing by splitting off is coupled and enhanced by usually highly rigid and ritualized forms of interactions which are maintained by brief and stereotyped verbal commands and threats (Furniss, 1991, p. 25).

Secondly, the experience creates two entirely opposite persons in one; this new 'other person' indulges in 'changed gestures, unusual speaking pattern, altered tone of voice and strange physical behaviour', not the least frightening of which is the dramatic changes in his facial expressions. The child cannot relate these changes to the sexual penetration accompanying them; as if, says Furniss, the abuser looks at the suffering face of the child and says, 'What do you mean, nothing is happening, is it?'

Thirdly the abuser facilitates this transformation from father into the 'other person' and vice versa by establishing 'entrance and exit rituals'.

These represent the high point of the cunning, deception and self-control of the perpetrator; they also constitute the most psychologically disorientating aspect of the abuse. The abuser interacts normally and innocently with the child at some innocuous moment, for example, genuinely enquiring about the netball match from which she's just returned; then he will manipulate the child in whatever way best facilitates the abuse (the entrance ritual), then carry out the abuse, and just as confidently extricate both himself and the child from the abusing situation (the exit ritual), and revert to the normality and innocence of the preceding interactions:

> Entrance and exit rituals do not only further reinforce the undoing and negation of sexual abuse in its very process. They also reinforce the powerful splitting of the contradictory physiological sensory messages during the abuse itself . . . they extend the incongruent experience of external reality into the dimension of time (Furniss, 1991, p. 26).

The likely educational and social consequences of this form of emotional and psychological abuse are documented in Caroline's case history in Chapter 5. In effect, Furniss substantiates the core points in our definitions of emotional and psychological abuse, and his analysis of the damage done to *perception* in particular is illuminating. But further comment is warranted on two other 'psychological casualties': morality and memory.

Attack on moral development

We have seen in the work of Harris (1989) how children at the earliest age develop a sense of right and wrong, and can actually prioritize acts in terms of how seriously they infringe moral and conventional codes of conduct. Socialization, education and family life can sharpen and strengthen, or weaken and blunt, the moral sense. At some point in time, a child of Caroline's age, reared by seemingly law-abiding, morally righteous, hardworking parents, is certain to awaken to the magnitude of the immorality of her father's actions. Impelled by the realization that such actions are not just immoral, but criminal, harmful and dependent upon an elaborate web of deceit, she will cry out in whatever way she can; her father, of course, has anticipated his daughter's thoughts and actions, and has implemented many strategies which gag her and compel her to dwell on terrible calamities should she indeed cry out. This is the beginning of the attack on both the child's moral sense and upon her conformity to generally accepted, strongly held views and feelings about the inappropriateness of sexual contact between an adult and a child, or worse, between a father and daughter. It is the beginning of the compromises which the child is forced to make, intensifying her sense of guilt, making her feel responsible for the abuse, and then graduating to the more serious levels of denial that the abuse has actually taken place, and, worst of all, being prepared to lie in defence of her abuser. Without help, any child in this position will have no option but to deceive by lying and/or denying. This erosion of moral sense will be accelerated by the attitude of the mother. The more indifferent or dismissive mother is to the cry for help, the more convinced the child becomes in the 'unbelievability' of her allegation, and/or of the catastrophic consequences should she attempt to persuade people to believe it (i.e. similar to the thoughts of the sexually abused boys in 'Kincora'; see Chapter 4). She will eventually be absorbed, consciously and unconsciously, by the web of deception spun by her father, and will make her own contribution to sustaining it. Moral development, i.e. the development of the moral sense and respect for conventional moral codes of contact, will be greatly impaired.

Memory: The enemy within

It is, ironically, the indestructibility and effectiveness of memory which enables it to function as a highly destructive force in older children who have been sexually abused. The memory of such abuse, and its associated pain, may be repressed, i.e. 'thrust out of consciousness into the unconscious'; yet it can still influence, and be the cause of, sexual, emotional and psychological difficulties in later life. Here we are looking at the more immediate effects of memory, its potential for unpredictable, uncontrollable 'retrieving' of minute details of the sexual abuse, including the intense physical arousal and pain, the disorientating contradictions, the smells (pleasant or sickening), the suffocation, the threats and violence, and the internal bodily sensations when anal or vaginal penetration is first perpetrated. Not least, it will recall those terrifying moments of realization of what 'my loving father' was really about, and the failure of the non-abusing parent to protect. Memory functions more accurately and effectively when 'retrieving' stressful incidents (Goodman *et al.*, 1991); the implication is that the more stressful, the more detailed will be the experiences 'retrieved'.

There can be another psychologically damaging consequence of effective memory: hatred, and a desire for revenge. This is very prevalent in cases where the abuser is a lately arrived stepfather or cohabitant. This has major implications for any therapy which may be offered to the child. Memory is not damaged or impaired as are other mental faculties and processes by psychological abuse; yet in its increased effectiveness, it can subject the child to nightmarish, repetitive and uncontrollable reliving of the original abuse. Though not impaired, memory temporarily ceases to function as the indispensable servant to other mental faculties and processes, particularly intelligence, perception and attention; in effect, it becomes the enemy of mental faculties and processes, a powerful elusive enemy within, often sabotaging the efforts of therapists to enable the child to recover from the abuse.

Agency responses to child sexual abuse

The psychological and emotional abuse unwittingly perpetrated by child protection agencies and police, in cases of suspected child sexual abuse, has been well documented (e.g. Butler-Sloss, 1988; Underwager and Wakefield, 1989; Brown, 1991) and commented upon *ad infinitum* in the media and in social work literature. Two problems are immediately apparent. First, many unwarranted interventions and removals of children who have *not* been sexually abused have lacked systematic, vigilant observations. Once again, classroom teachers are best equipped to make such observations, and any intervention which takes place without consulting and fully involving them in the assessment process is as negligent as it is inadequate. It is inconceivable that Caroline would not have been sending her teacher some signals of distress and/or poor work performance. Secondly, interventions in cases where children *have* been sexually abused will be disastrous (in terms of the emotional and psychological abuse they inflict on the child) if they succeed in uniting the abusing and non-abusing parent and turning the latter against the child (O'Hagan, 1989). That will strengthen the perpetrator's resolve to deny the abuse, diminish the likelihood of a successful prosecution, and ensure greater psychological harm.

Post-intervention: The victim–perpetrator relationship

It is not within the scope of this text to address the issue of strategies and therapies for working with sexually abused children; however, there is a developing expertise which is achieving much success in this area (e.g. Wyatt and Powell, 1988; Harper, 1989; Gomes-Schartz *et al.*, 1990; Furniss, 1991). But there is one neglected aspect of the problem which has enormous potential for sabotaging progress generally, and the child's continuing psychological health in particular. This refers to the relationship between child and perpetrator, and the feelings and perceptions the former has of the latter. There will be many occasions when the child's feelings, memories and perceptions of the perpetrator will be major obstacles in the path of therapy. What is happening to the perpetrator may be a major preoccupation for the child. Caroline may or may not have wanted her father to have 'been removed': if she feared that prospect, and it occurred, the psychological damage already done may be compounded by guilt; if she desperately wanted him removed, and it was decided that he couldn't be removed for want of evidence, then the psychological damage will be compounded by fear and helplessness. Experience in this particular aspect of child sexual abuse convinces me that there are less psychological complications and more therapeutic potential when the perpetrator is successfully prosecuted, even though this is not what the child desires at the time. Such an outcome, however, depends fundamentally upon *a highly professional investigation and intervention in the first instance, which has ensured that the non-abusing parent remains supportive of the child.* That support, plus therapy, plus time, can alleviate the child of guilt; even more effective in achieving this objective may be the perpetrator's attitude and willingness to see the child.

It will be obvious now that there are very many variables affecting outcome in the victim–perpetrator relationship (for a fuller discussion, see Mrazek and Mrazek, 1981; Gomes-Schartz *et al.*, 1990). In the case of a successful prosecution and conviction leading to a custodial sentence, the therapeutic potential mentioned can be realized in the child being given the opportunity to confront the abuser to hear him/her confess to their crime, express their guilt, sorrow and remorse, and to accept full responsibility for the abuse. Counselling, group therapy, self-protective games and exercises, all of these may be crucial to the child's recovery and future protection; but the child, if willing, should be given the opportunity to meet the perpetrator. Of course, it also depends upon the perpetrator admitting the offence, and being prepared to face the child; 'very few are' may be the relieved and unanimous cry. But it depends upon the willingness of professionals to explore this matter, to contemplate its therapeutic potential, meet the perpetrator, to maintain contact, to offer counselling, and to enable him/her eventually to face up and acknowledge that even though the abuse is long past, the emotional and psychological damage remains. Unfortunately, many child care professionals are content to see the perpetrator out of sight and out of mind, convinced that that's what's best for everyone involved. But the child whose nightmares and miseries continue well into their adult years may begin to think differently at some point, for numerous reasons. For example, it may be because the child has had no contact with the perpetrator, has not seen him/her behind prison walls, has not heard him/her admit and express *genuine* remorse for what has been done to her – therein lies the danger of a swelling hatred and bitterness based on a conviction that he/she now roams free, utterly indifferent to the crime (because so few perpetrators are actually prosecuted, this possibility has to be given serious consideration). As police methods improve and all the relevant agencies liaise more effectively in mounting their investigation and intervention, there are likely to be more admissions of guilt by perpetrators. The Home Office's recent announcement on treatment for offenders should also help. Child care professionals in general must begin *at least thinking* about the therapeutic potential of the child confronting the perpetrator. Even though enormous preparation is necessary, and due attention must be given to matters like location, duration, protection and atmosphere, professionals can be reassured by the fact that if the child is not given such an opportunity, therein lies the prospect of the festering psychological wounding, its greatest pain caused not least by a memory fuelling the already debilitating hatred and revenge.

Summary and conclusions

This chapter has concentrated upon four categories of emotionally and psychologically abused children. Clear patterns of behaviour and/or emotional expressivity and/or psychological malfunctioning will be discernible in any of these cases, and detailed, systematic observation is of paramount importance. Some frameworks have been provided to assist in the observational task. Assessment of the emotional life of infants is inadequate without sufficient interactions between them and the professional assessors. The exposure of widespread sexual abuse has further inhibited professionals in interacting sufficiently with infants. The psychological abuse of some older children of alcoholic and mentally ill parents often generates a crisis in the neighbourhood which necessitates community crisis intervention. The child will greatly welcome this initial wider focus, as a potent source of the psychological abuse lies within the child's realization of how the parent is perceived, feared and despised by the community. It is imperative that the child knows and can see that the professional will make every effort to help the parent. No matter what effort has been made on the parent's behalf, however, some alcoholic and mentally ill parents may not be able to provide adequate care for their children. The life of the emotionally abused older child is often characterized by negative emotion, bizarre behaviour, difficulty in communicating and socializing, and physical abuse. Tactful, systematic and detailed observations of child–carer(s) interactions are crucial. So, too, may be observation of material factors highly significant to the child e.g. locks on the bedroom door, discarded drawings which nobody looked at, etc. Communication with the emotionally abused older child can be extremely difficult. Much patience, tolerance and persistence will be required. Older children who are repeatedly sexually abused by a natural parent in particular, often endure massive psychological and emotional abuse. The more cunning the abuser and the more effective the web of deceit, the greater will be the emotional and psychological damage. The moral sense and memory of the child are two significant psychological components which will be seriously affected by sexual abuse. The relationship between victim and perpetrator, and the feelings and perceptions which the latter has for the former, will also be important considerations in post-intervention work.

8

THE EMOTIONAL AND PSYCHOLOGICAL ABUSE OF MICHELLE

Introduction

This chapter will concentrate on a single case of emotional and psychological abuse. Comment will be provided on significant factors during and after each phase of child protection work, i.e. referral, investigation, intervention, case conference and court proceedings. Although the case occurred some years ago, significant events, problems encountered and actions taken will be described in the context of the implementation of the Children Act 1989, with particular emphasis upon (1) the concepts of 'significant harm', (2) 'protection' and 'care' and (3) rehabilitation. The same principle of anonymity which has applied in the use of other case material will be rigorously applied in this one; because of the necessary detail of description and analysis, material factors have been substantially altered, but proceedings and outcome are exactly as described.

The referral

The nursery teacher, Kay, was quite brilliant. This was no random referral, no quick-fix anxiety relief late on a Friday afternoon. Her referral came in the middle of the week, calmly, confidently; she had been watching Michelle over many days; she had taken a keen interest; she had negotiated with one of her colleagues to have Michelle placed in her group; she worked hard at engaging her; she then began her systematic recording of observations; she recorded how she saw her on arrival each day, how she played and related, what she was like at meal-time, toilet-time, break-time, and at the end of the day when she was collected. Then she discussed with her Officer in Charge, who phoned social services and gave the following details.

Michelle was nearly three years of age. She had been attending the nursery for two months. She arrived each nursery day with any one of five or six persons, though the predominant person was her aunt, sister of her mother. Michelle was often dirty and smelly, though this was no exception in the nursery. The arrivals each morning were totally devoid of any kind of warmth or enthusiasm on the part of the aunt. Michelle initially seemed interested, and would run from her aunt, barely giving her time to get the coat off; but, eventually, the child's response on getting to the nursery mirrored her aunt's – an apparently disinterested, lethargic approach.

In the nursery, Michelle seldom smiled. Her emotional range seemed limited. As Kay read out the exciting stories and the children's eyes riveted on her, Michelle seemed unmoved. Meal-time revealed her inability to use a spoon and fork; she was least conscious of the mess she created. Toilet training was a major problem; she could be persuaded to sit on a potty, but taking her to the toilet provoked massive resistance, she remained in nappies. She became increasingly conspicuous in isolation. She just did not respond to the other children as they wanted her to, and as Kay expected her to; even the infectious, rapturous giggles of her particular group could not elicit much response from her; she was handicapped with a severely restricted vocabulary, some 15–20 words, more that of a child half her age; it seemed as though she found it difficult to speak. She never talked to herself in play, like the other children; she seemed incapable of the use of pronouns 'I' and 'me'; she seldom expressed any curiosity in play, never asking questions, like what? why? and where? Her concentration and attentiveness was significantly lower than that of any other child. She became silent and withdrawn though not, thought Kay, indifferent: Kay felt she still retained some interest in the world around her, though it may only have been a painful preoccupation with her predicament in it; in other words, she seemed conscious of her misery and her increasing isolation.

Break-time and the nursery playground seemed particularly challenging to her; she never ran about freely like the other children; she ran rather nervously and unevenly; she had great difficulty in kicking a ball, and she could not steer or drive the tricycles; she gradually found her way to wherever Kay was, and remained there. Any attempt to encourage her to play with the other children failed. Kay could not always be with her. Occasionally, some of the children themselves tried to engage her; they failed too. The less charitable made no such effort; they became resentful and hostile towards her; they bullied and humiliated her, and when they saw some status mileage in the response of others, they intensified the bullying and humiliation. It was then that Kay observed behaviour in Michelle which alarmed her. Michelle appeared to accept the bullying, i.e. she never tried to get out of the way; she didn't fight back; she didn't even resist; it was disturbing to watch her being hit repeatedly by a number of children; sometimes they kicked her, and she just stood there, seemingly emotionless, and the attackers were as much baffled as they were infuriated by this lack of response, which provoked them into more vicious attacks. Kay would rescue her then, take her to one side, wanting to comfort her; but Michelle froze, as if it was no comfort at all; there were no tears, no anger, no aggression, no expression of any kind. Kay was convinced that Michelle was profoundly unhappy and disturbed.

Kay attempted to talk to Mrs Bell, Michelle's aunt. Mrs Bell hadn't a clue what Kay was talking about. She was herself severely limited in speech. She said that Michelle was 'driving her mad'; that she was most often 'bad', deliberately so; she 'couldn't get through to her', she said, 'nobody seemed able to get through to her'. And it wasn't fair she was landed with this responsibility; she had never asked for it, she was just trying to help. Besides, she had her own problems: she had three teenage children, a semi-invalid, alcoholic husband, and no money. Why didn't somebody think of trying to help her?

Comment

There is nothing exceptional in the detail of observation by the nursery teacher; perhaps her taking the trouble to record it is not so common. We have frequently been reminded in previous chapters of the key assessment role of classroom/nursery teachers, particularly in cases of suspected emotional and psychological abuse. Social workers in particular have got to accept the primacy of the teacher's role in the initial stages of assessment. For those teachers who have not recorded the detail of their observations, the social worker has the responsibility of exploring all the areas comprehensively covered in the referral above, i.e. speech, play, extent of emotional expressivity, dominant emotional expressivity, social integration, intelligence, perception (particularly of self), attention and moral sense. Teachers invariably observe the consequences of emotional and psychological abuse. The social worker then has to seek the causes.

Investigation

Preliminary investigations revealed the following: Michelle was the oldest child of Mary, 21. Michelle's father, Alex, had never seen her; his

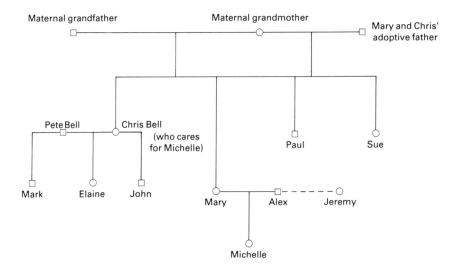

Figure 8.1   Family genogram

whereabouts were unknown. Mary then cohabited with Jeremy, aged 30. Mary was the second eldest of four children – Chris, 28 (the aunt who brought Michelle to the nursery), Paul, 19, and Sue, 16. Mary and Chris had been adopted by the natural father of Paul and Sue. Their own father and mother – the mother of all four children – separated when Mary was two and Chris was nine; they never saw their father after that. Chris had three children, Mark, 10, Elaine, 9, and John, 7. The family genogram is shown in Fig. 8.1.

Files recorded numerous agencies' involvement with the three generations of the family going back more than twenty years. The reasons for involvement were poverty, destitution, allegations of neglect, complaints by neighbours, homelessness, physical abuse (of Chris and Mary), special education (of all four children), care proceedings in respect of Chris and Mary, residential homes, abscondings and, more recently, concerns expressed by health visitors about the care of Michelle. There was also the details of an investigation into allegations of sexual abuse of Mary by her adoptive father when she was fourteen. He admitted to some of the charges and was cautioned; Mary was taken into care and soon absconded. There were many admissions to residential homes and just as many abscondings. She returned home on occasions, but found the situation intolerable. She eventually met Alex, and lived with him; however, the relationship soon degenerated into constant rows and violence – Mary was beaten up repeatedly. Michelle was born and the relationship never improved. Alex left, and Mary ended up in a hostel.

There was no information available about the most recent past, about the whereabouts of Mary; nor was there any explanation why Chris, the eldest sister of Mary, had apparently assumed responsibility for Michelle. Now it was time to visit the home of Chris, to see child and carer together, to look at the family, social and environmental contexts, and to explore the possibility of 'significant harm' clearly indicated in the observations made at the nursery (Children Act 1989, s. 47(1)(b)).

First contact

My visit was timely. Michelle's aunt Chris had beaten her for not eating her dinner and turning her plate over on the table. She had lifted the child and carried her up the stairs, and locked her in the bedroom. I asked Chris if I could see Michelle; Chris was in such a mood of exasperation that she couldn't have cared less. Like Kay, the nursery teacher, I too found it difficult to understand Chris; it seemed she had a chronic speech impediment. She remained in her armchair. She chain-smoked compulsively. I left the tiny living room and made for the stairs; I noticed the single bed which dominated the living room, obviously a convenience for either Chris or her husband. In one corner, there was a gigantic ancient black-and-white television; Chris sat two feet away from it. There was a settee, heavily stained, with no cushions; mugs of cold tea were scattered around. In another corner there were newspapers and dirty clothes piled in a heap.

The staircase was narrow and dark. The clatter of each step on cold uncovered floorboards seemed accentuated by darkness. I worried that my strange footsteps would be instantly recognized by the child and that she would either come running to the door, or maybe panic and scream, and hide under the bed. On the other hand, I had this terrible thought that Chris may have beaten her black and blue – maybe she was unconscious now!

The bolt was placed near the top of the door, well out of any child's reach. It looked a fragile door, huge chunks of its covering plywood missing. The imprint of kicks covered the bottom of it; the centre was full of scores, drawings done with crayons, and various forms of filth. I unlocked the bolt and opened it, and walked into a far more impenetrable darkness; it was quite a few seconds before my eyes could adjust.

Michelle lay half covered with filthy sheets; she was facing me and made neither noise nor move. I was convinced she was sound asleep, and I was relieved; perhaps she's only got a good telling off. But as I moved closer to the bed I had this uncomfortable realization that she wasn't asleep; I stopped and stared at her for a while, still trying to focus and make sense in the ghastly, stench-laden darkness. I was about two metres from her now, and I could see two large, wide-awake eyes following every move I made. It was precisely that second when I felt the darkness to be insufferable, and I was no longer inhibited about the possible impacts of whatever movements I made in the room. Surprisingly, unnervingly, I a male stranger had entered this room and made many movements and this child appeared to react with the utmost indifference. I hastily pulled the thick heavy curtain material back from the window; the windows were filthy and sealed shut with the effects of grime and condensation; but the light made an enormous difference, and I returned to the bedside, got down on my knees, and looked at Michelle. Normally, like every other worker, I may have indulged in friendly toddler talk; or I may have attempted the more subtle tactic of pretending I was ignoring her, then engaging in some activity that she herself could not ignore, like doing a funny drawing, or commenting upon and reaching out to something that would have been important to her. Such tactics were irrelevant at this moment. Michelle was allowing me the opportunity to observe and to concentrate, without the distracting task of justifying my existence to her; but her behaviour none the less – those large and beautiful wide-awake eyes, following me, staring into my own eyes – left a deep and lasting impression upon me.

Eventually, I spoke to her. My voice startled her; it didn't frighten her, it merely took her by surprise and it interested her. She lay for a few moments, as if contemplating me and my voice, then she thrust the sheets away and stretched up, and said something in reply; I could not understand, though it was obviously something of importance to her. I spoke to her again; she gave another incomprehensible reply, pure baby talk it was, and she further raised herself from the bed. She was fully clothed with socks and shoes still on. There were fresh dinner stains on her too-tight green dress and on her face. Her hair was long but lifeless, unclean; there was not the slightest indication that she had been sleeping; it seemed as though she had been just lying there, silently, without protest or tears; and it seemed too that even if some playful toys had lain all around her, she would not have played. I suggested as best I could that she accompany me down to the living room. I offered her my hand. She didn't seem to understand, and I reached out and held her gently, and moved towards the door. She never resisted, nor did she display any fear. She never looked up at me. She walked unsteadily alongside me, trusting me or indifferent to me. I repeatedly spoke to her, in an effort to reassure her, but there was no need to, she would have walked anywhere with me, or with anybody else for that matter. Whatever had been done to Michelle had also made her the sexual abuser's dream-child! (see Chapter 3 on how damage to perception renders the child particularly vulnerable to abusers).

Exploring and assessing the quality of caring

Chris's armchair was curiously positioned in a way that ensured she had a monopoly on watching the television; anyone coming into the room would see the back of the armchair, then Chris's head, and then the huge television screen above. It was as if she wanted to immerse herself in television as a means of locking out the world behind her. Part of that awful world was 'caring for Michelle'. Chris never budged when we entered. The television blared. Then she looked sideways, and seeing our blurred images through the side of her eye, she made some grunting noise, supposed to be a greeting; but she had no inclination to turn her seat round and face us; she would have been happy for me to walk on and through and out of the house altogether. I requested she turn the television off so that we might chat; another grunting sound. She then contorted herself to look round; I suggested she manoeuvred the chair round so that she didn't have to strain her neck; her expression implied that I had requested something akin to demolishing the house!

Two things struck me immediately, first about Chris herself and, secondly, about the interactions between her and the child. She seemed to be an enormously damaged person in many ways; the major speech difficulty must have caused serious social problems in her upbringing. She was not inhibited or shy about her speech; indeed, when she was expressing strong feelings about Michelle she talked ceaselessly, she just couldn't help talking incomprehensively. Secondly, her emotional range was extremely narrow and this became apparent in her interactions with Michelle, but it was also a problem unto herself; severely limited speech and emotion in the carer was not exactly conducive to providing for the child. Chris really hadn't a clue about the latter. She looked at Michelle a few times; she wasn't angry or exasperated anymore, and she didn't seem to be a vindictive person who might loathe and hold the child responsible for my interfering visit. She seemed to have forgotten what Michelle had done to her dinner; she had many other preoccupations.

Michelle stood resolutely beside me as I gave Chris some more details about the nursery's concerns, and enquired about the whereabouts of Mary, the child's mother. With difficulty I learnt that this caring arrangement was by no means permanent. Mary 'came and went when it was convenient for her' said Chris. 'Convenient' meant that Mary cared for Michelle in the home of her new cohabitant, Jeremy, only so long as she wasn't being beaten up. When she was beaten up, she would come and 'dump' Michelle on Chris, and 'walk the streets' until someone took her in. Mary had been in and out of all kinds of places, Chris said. I enquired about the number of times this dumping of Michelle had occurred; Chris said at least once every two to three weeks.

'Why do you let yourself be used as the dumping ground?' I asked.

'Somebody has to take her', she replied.

'Does she pay you?'

She made a contemptuous sound: 'only when she feels like it'.

'Doesn't she realize what's she's doing?'

Chris was inhaling one of her cigarettes when I asked that question; it gave me the briefest moment to realize how risky a question it was. I thought I should withdraw it, but then I thought that whatever Chris may say now in the child's presence was certain to be infinitely less than that said by either her or Mary in my absence.

'She hate's her', Chris replied.

Michelle never moved; her staring elsewhere remained fixed; her tiny warm hand, still clasped in my hand, betrayed neither understanding nor hurt. Still, I was furious with myself for asking the question!

A colleague and I later returned to the home to meet Chris's family, her semi-invalid, alcoholic husband, and her three children, Mark, Elaine and John. Chris's term of 'dumping' Michelle was appropriate. We could see no indication of any integration of the child into the family. There was no sign of bonding, nor any special relationship. The three children led their own separate lives, of which Michelle had no part; they came and went, their friends too, having no more contact with Michelle than was necessary through bumping into her, finding her in their way. It should be acknowledged, however, that these children had little physical or emotional contact with their parents either; they had adapted well to their parents' limitations and were heavily dependent upon their school lives, peer groups and adventures outside. Michelle was not so lucky; Chris was her principal carer, severely limited in speech, mobility and emotional expressivity. She was neither intelligent nor sensitive in her attitude and behaviour towards Michelle, and therefore unlikely to be able to understand let alone provide for the child's needs.

Witnessing the abuse

We traced Michelle's mother, Mary, and her cohabitant Jeremy, to a dingy tenement block in another part of the city. We thought that she would have been informed on the grapevine about the social services involvement, and were curious as to its impact. Had we called with Chris before setting out to meet Mary, we would have realized it had significant impact: she panicked and removed Michelle! Not an untypical response from a young mother anticipating the worst from a dreaded social worker (see the case of Rani in Chapters 5 and 6).

We heard Michelle's screams as we walked along the littered balcony of the tenement block. Experience told us these were not the screams of a child being battered. I knocked on the door, but there was no reply (we didn't really expect a reply!). My colleague opened the door and shouted along the narrow hallway; the door at the far end of the hall was half open; we felt a part of the violence now. It wouldn't stop; they either didn't hear us or they were ignoring us. We moved along the hallway, speedily, apprehensively and, some may believe, illegally; we were both conscious of the risks, but we were far more conscious of the screams of a child whom we knew had already endured prolonged and damaging abuse. (I have interrupted family violence on many occasions before, and always anticipated the worst, but it hasn't happened to date. I believe that the interruption is often welcome. Apart from the acute embarrassment felt by one or other family members, at least one of them will welcome the breaking of the vicious cycle of violence which they have created amongst themselves and are helpless in controlling. I would not recommend to any readers that they behave similarly, but I would stress the professional and moral compulsion which many child care professionals will feel in these situations, to rescue and protect.)

Jeremy, a man of about 30, six feet tall, stood towering over Michelle's mother. She was pinned between a small cabinet and the chimney breast while he was flailing into her with his fists. She was attempting to scratch at his eyes and kick at his shins; he roared and she screamed. Michelle was at the opposite end of the room. She was on an armchair, trying to bury herself in one corner of it. Her tiny arms clutched a large filthy doll, which, because of her terror and tension, was being systematically mangled. It was as if the child was trying to squeeze and crush the nightmare before her out of existence, or, possibly, trying to bring about her own non-existence. I have seldom seen a child's face with such anguish; there were no tears, just a combination of acute pain and terror; I could see no physical cause of the pain.

Within seconds, the scene was transformed. We were not attacked. We had identity cards in our hands, but they were not needed. Jeremy had exhausted himself in his attack upon Mary, and realized who we were; he was more apprehensive than us. Mary made a surrendering gesture by just collapsing in a heap and weeping profusely. My colleague immediately moved towards Michelle to comfort her. I could not help myself, saying to Jeremy: 'We're here to see the child's okay . . . do you think she looks okay?'

I didn't expect a reply, and I was confident the irony would not provoke. We stayed with the couple for a long time after; we learnt a great deal about both of them and their tortuous relationship. But as far as the abuse of Michelle was concerned, we had learnt more in the first second of our visit than we might learn in anything seen and heard thereafter.

Comment

Chaos, violence, impermanency and fragmentation are commonly found in the families of emotionally and psychologically abused children. Previously, we have analysed in detail what the terms mean, and have examined each of the many separate consequences of such abuse. But there is a ghastly wholeness about the abuse endured by Michelle, which we must try to grasp. This wholeness is not just in respect of the innumerable manifestations of the abuse, but, more importantly, as perceived by the child herself. Vernon (1962) writes: 'A further difficulty for the young child is that he tends to perceive situations as a whole' (p. 21). In Michelle's case, the perception is the reality. The carers' behaviour towards her, whether it be sustained, repetitive, inappropriate emotional responses, or repeatedly locking her away in the dank and dark filthy bedroom (with all its consequences of the child's psychological development), or, worst of all, her witnessing the systematic battering of her mother, these are mere symptoms of a blanket wholeness of abuse daily perpetrated against her. In only a few contacts with the child and those entrusted with her care, Michelle gave every indication that she perceived no other contrasting world where she might have been treated differently. Her apathy and surrender in her dungeon of a bedroom, and her sufferance of attacks by other children in the nursery, are particularly revealing of a child with no hope or expectation that her lot may improve. The chaotic, unplanned alternating care, from a mother being repeatedly battered, to an aunt overladen with her own domestic and personal responsibilities (and neither aunt nor uncle having the slightest clue as to the child's needs), could only reinforce Michelle's worst perceptions of a cruel and incomprehensible world around her, and of her helplessness in doing anything about it.

Confronting the abuser

A few days later, I visited Jeremy. He told me he was finished with Mary. (Mary had said the same, but I was not convinced.) I told him that matter was not the reason for my visit. Whether he liked it or not I wanted to talk to him about Michelle, about what I believed his attacks upon her mother had done to the child. I asked him to tell me what *he thought* his attacks upon Mary had done to Michelle. What did he think Michelle was feeling that moment we entered his home? Could he remember the expression on her face? Had he ever given any thought to how she might feel the next day? Did he ever think he was harming her in any way? Did he ever feel sorry for what he had done?

Predictably, Jeremy indulged in ceaseless excuse making, revolving around how insufferingly fiendish Mary was to him! Each time he did this, I acknowledged the fact that I did not know who was responsible for their rows, nor was I interested at this point in time; I merely wanted him to give me answers to the questions I asked about Michelle. He couldn't answer, but I could tell from the look on his face that he *sensed* the damage he had done. I told him what we had learnt about Michelle from the nursery; I told him of our own observations of her; I said that it had all been very mysterious to us until that moment when we stumbled upon the child terrorized because her mother was getting the life punched out of her. If this was typical of their relationship, I said, there was no mystery about Michelle's miserable existence. Jeremy exploded, again entirely predictably, and cursed and fumed about that 'f.....g witch!' I listened to him for a long time. It was quite some time before he was able to acknowledge that this explosiveness had nothing to do with Mary; it was merely an expression of his own guilt.

Comment

I have never been able to accept that those who batter women and inflict terrible emotional and psychological damage upon children, as a consequence are least seen, heard and challenged about their actions. This relationship between Mary and Jeremy seemed at an end, so why, one may ask, risk provocation by confronting the batterer? The question to me is as nonsensical as ignoring the batterer. Any individual who engages in this obscenity should at least be enlightened about why it's an obscenity. They should be enlightened in whatever way is appropriate, about the possible connections between their behaviour and the misery of the child. That may be as above, in one-to-one conversation; it can be direct, indirect, or very subtle; it may refer to research or experience, the worker's or the batterer's; it may even involve inviting the batterer to talk to nursery staff, to see and point out the child's conspicuously distressed behaviour. If this is too threatening, or impossible, then one can write to him. The printed word, provided sufficient care has been taken, can be even more powerful in its effect. My reason for emphasizing this task is two-fold.

First, it is a necessary part of the continuous assessment of certain aspects of the case; but, secondly, one enlightens the batterer in the hope that it minimizes the risk of similar damage being perpetrated to the children he lives with in the future. To make him aware of the emotionally and psychologically damaging consequences suffered by the child (by whatever language or explanatory tactic it takes to drive the message home), to stress the illegality and immorality of it, and to make it clear that it cannot be tolerated, is surely the least effort that can be made on behalf of those children of the future. Forgetting about people like Jeremy is convenient; but it's hardly indicative of professional responsibility.

Examination, continuous assessment and strategy

Michelle was examined by a paediatrician and speech therapist. The paediatrician later diagnosed non-organic failure-to-thrive, and said it also looked like a case of severe neglect. The speech therapist confirmed a major retardation in speech development. My colleague and I, and the health visitor and nursery teacher, diagnosed emotional and psychological abuse on the basis of our shared observations and experiences with Michelle and her carers. Intensive research and consultation took place between all the professionals involved and with Michelle's mother. Mary had cooperated with these preliminary professional assessments, but she remained somewhat traumatized as a consequence of the recent battering, being without a permanent home, and now subjected to what she perceived as 'bloody interference' by social workers. She was not receptive to our offer of accommodation for both herself and Michelle. She left Michelle with Chris again, then disappeared, but not before declaring she would fight any attempt to 'take my kid off me!'.

Comment

Mary's behaviour was neither unreasonable nor entirely unpredictable. She was unlikely, in her crisis state, to realize that leaving Michelle once again with Chris, suddenly and ill-prepared, was merely a continuation of the impermanency and confusion to which the child had been subjected. But, as the Children Act rightly stresses, it is imperative for workers to make every effort to gain and sustain the parent's understanding and cooperation throughout intervention, to offer whatever 'advice, guidance and counselling' may be necessary or helpful in enabling parent and child to remain together, and to realize that any continuous assessment without the parent is incomplete (see ss. 17 and 20; and Schedule 2:4(1); 8 (a)). The assessments made by numerous professionals clearly indicated that the child had been, and was being, 'significantly harmed'. The questions which now arose were: Did such assessments warrant application for authority to remove the child? And, was it in the child's interests to do nothing until mother turned up again?

Case conference

A case conference was held. The details of the assessments were shared. Michelle's name was placed on the child protection register. Conference endorsed the following recommendations for action: (1) rescue and protection; (2) further assessment of the emotional and psychological damage done and of its social and behavioural consequences; (3) regular and frequent contact between mother and child, and assessment of the relationship between them (we were confident she would eventually return); (4) exploring Mary's perceptions and feelings about the abuses Michelle had suffered; (5) assessment of the potential for rehabilitation between mother and child, and empowering the former by whatever 'advice, guidance and counselling' was appropriate, and offering practical help that would be conducive to the rehabilitation. The Children Act is quite specific about the types of empowering supports local authorities should provide in order to reduce the need for care proceedings or, if the child is apart from her parent, in order to reunite them (see Schedule 2:8(a)–(e); 9(1)–(3); 10(a)(b)).

An interesting development then occurred, indicative of some of the obstacles to the consideration of emotional and psychological factors in child care, which have been mentioned in earlier chapters. The department's legal adviser was doubtful about convincing the court that the child's development was being seriously impaired by emotional and psychological abuse, and was not confident, therefore, that a Place of Safety Order would be granted. But during the period when this issue was being discussed, the nursery made a referral about bruising found on Michelle – non-accidental injury was confirmed by a doctor. Chris admitted hitting her, and was terrified of the consequences. Numerous attempts were made again to contact Mary, but without success. Our legal adviser had no hesitation then in pursuing 'protection', but on the grounds of physical abuse! My colleague and I negotiated a placement for Michelle. She was taken to the home of Mrs Sullivan (Kath), a single parent of exceptional quality and experience.

Comment

The Children Act ensures that the emotional and psychological health of the child, and any factors which impede or impair that health, are firmly on the agenda of any assessment, and referred to in applications to the court. The reluctance of child care solicitors to acknowledge this fact is understandable; they are steeped in a tradition of applications invariably based upon evidence of various types of physical or sexual abuse. This reluctance can eventually be overcome by workers from *all* the child care agencies providing detailed, systematic and accurate observations of other aspects of the child's welfare, and being confident in addressing their observations while on the witness stand. In Michelle's case (as in so many others), the battering she received in one particular incident was less significant than the cumulative effects of the prolonged emotional and psychological abuse she had suffered.

Mother's return

Not surprisingly, the mother who could not be found turned up a few days after Michelle's admission to foster home. My colleague and I welcomed her. We could see she expected us to criticize her; she gave the impression of anxiety and defensiveness, as if she were ready to attack us should we dare to criticize her. We told her we were sorry to hear things had apparently got worse; we hoped we could talk to her to see if there was any way in which we might help. She did not demand Michelle's return, merely her whereabouts, and the chance to see her; all her anger (and no small amount of guilt) was concentrated on her sister Chris for causing the injuries to her child, which was understandable, but neither fair nor helpful.

Our profile of Mary was far from complete, but she was significantly different from Chris in appearance, intelligence and personality. Her face bore the signs of previous batterings, a factor which caused us much unease. She was reasonably articulate, and very preoccupied with her early past (on which she blamed all her present woes). Surprisingly, she agreed with the department's action, saying that she was not yet in a position to care for Michelle. She wanted reassurance that Michelle would not be taken off her permanently. She was in effect acknowledging that Michelle had been badly treated; more importantly, she was indicating a potential for understanding how, and the consequences.

We told her we'd be pleased to take her to Michelle, and we stressed our appreciation of her patience. We gave her the name and address of the foster mother, but asked her not to make contact until we'd had an opportunity to arrange introductions. We were confident that she would respect that. We would contact the foster mother Kath, and we'd arrange for her to see Michelle within the next few days, preferably at the nursery. Then, perhaps, we suggested, one of us might visit her own home, wherever that was at present (we did not press her to find out), and listen to whatever she had to tell us. We advised her there wasn't much point in thinking about wreaking revenge on her sister Chris; Chris after all had done her best, bailing Mary out of her difficulties on many occasions.

Comment

Mary, too, just like her sister Chris and some of the professionals, was greatly affected by the bruises inflicted on Michelle; it was, however, a convenient diversion distracting her and many others from the more serious abuse being inflicted upon Michelle. But she revealed some guilty awareness about this, a first promising hint of understanding and empathy with her child, whom she needed to see, and also, the person caring for her. The Children Act emphasizes much more than previous legislation the necessity of contact between parent and child (Schedule 2:15). In Michelle's case, rescue and protection from continuous emotional and psychological abuse necessitated temporary removal; the damage caused by such abuse necessitated a period of therapy and care. But it is precisely the seriousness of the abuse and the rapidity of intervention which necessitates frequent and regular contact between child and parent. There are two reasons: first, the very young child's contact with the parent (even the abusing parent) will minimize the inevitable trauma associated with the combination of abuse and removal; secondly, it will facilitate the assessment and rehabilitative tasks which must then be considered. Nothing is better calculated to sabotage assessment work and rehabilitation plans than denying a parent contact with her very young child, and denying her knowledge of the people you may consider more capable of caring for that child.

The child in the foster home

Kath, the foster mother, was too experienced to fall into the many pitfalls presented by the severely abused and damaged three-year-old. In her first contact with Michelle, Kath's communication consisted of nothing more than one-syllable sentences, nothing more than the child herself could utter or cope with. There was no demonstrative compassion, no taking the child on her knee and burying her face in the child's face with soothing, comforting words (an invariably compulsive gesture by less experienced professionals, unwittingly putting great pressure on the child). In the first few days in the foster home, she behaved towards Michelle in precisely the same way, but she engaged in various other 'stragegic' behaviours which were certain eventually to interest Michelle: conspicuously and noisily rocking to-and-fro on her beloved rocking chair; stroking her magnificent black cat as it poised itself on her knees; stretching out on the floor creating exquisite designs out of old newspapers; filling up jugs of water to place on her most valuable aid, the sand and water trolley (also the messiest!); or, safest of all, playing cartoon cassettes. It was a long haul for Kath, and quite a few days before Michelle felt safe enough to take any initiative. The very first initiative Kath reported was Michelle meekly gesturing with her eyes and head a request to have one of the cassettes shown. With Kath's tactful encouragement, that soon led to her being able to push the cassette in herself. Kath wisely refrained from too much praise, an experience totally alien to Michelle, and threatening in large doses. A more courageous initiative soon followed: she was fascinated by the movement and noise of the rocking chair, and she went closer to have a look. Then she uttered a sound that Kath could not understand but knew was a question. It was a significant breakthrough, not just mere curiosity, but expressing it; it would lead inevitably to the more daring initiative of climbing onto the rocking chair when Kath wasn't there; taking risks to satisfy her curiosity.

I noticed a substantial change within a week. Michelle's eyes were more alert and inquisitive; her skin was less taut; she was more mobile, unafraid of making noise or a mess. Mess she made aplenty, particularly with the water and sand; Kath said she spent hours pouring water and sand. I watched her on numerous occasions; she seemed captivated by the water, by its transparency and touch, by her ability to make it cascade or explode, stretch out or narrow to a trickle, spread noiselessly when she could hold it steadily, make a different noise and impact each time it fell onto a different surface, and turning sand into something totally different from sand. It was fascinating to watch her preoccupation with these endlessly repetitive experiments, creating her own time, space and achievements, taking massive leaps forward in perception, attention and intelligence; inevitably, language would flower too. At this point, her uninhibited, incomprehensible babble to herself was success enough, a far cry from the noiseless, emotionless, unhappy child in the nursery.

Comment

The severely emotionally and psychologically abused very young child may be helped in various ways. If that child is going to be separated from her parent or significant other person, it is necessary to place the child in the care of a highly skilled, dedicated, experienced foster parent. Major distractions, like numerous demanding family commitments, or a home where hard-pressed social workers have already placed four or five children (not uncommon in my experiences), should be totally unacceptable. Planning for the application to the court under the new legislation for an Emergency Protection Order (s. 44), an Assessment Order (including the authority for the child to be assessed away from home: s. 43(9)) or a Care Order (s. 31) necessitates consideration of the Welfare Principle (s. 1) and the declaration in s. 1(5):

'. . . the court shall not make the order or any of the orders unless it considers that doing so would be better for the child than making no order at all'. In other words, the court is likely to need convincing not just that the child is being harmed but also that the proposed alternative care is capable of undoing the harm. O'Hagan (1989) places the issue of 'resources' firmly within an ethical framework: it is unethical to remove a child from an abusing situation and place the child in an inadequate foster or residential home. The Children Act places resources generally and alternative accommodation in particular within a powerful legal framework. These ethical and legal contexts together must compel local authorities to provide the necessary and adequate care for children they seek to protect.

Implementing the strategy

A Care Order was eventually obtained. Space does not permit a recording of all the developments preceding and following the granting of that order: Mary's increasing stabilization and acquiring of accommodation; the termination of her relationship with Jeremy; the interim care hearings; and the regular reports of those assessing aspects of Michelle's development. But the following is a summary of significant events within the main components of strategy previously mentioned. The remainder of the chapter will then concentrate upon the objective of reuniting parent and child.

Continuous assessment of the child

No matter how great the extent of abuse which one discovers during an investigation, the foster parent caring for the child is certain to observe much more manifestation and consequence of that abuse. Strange men's voices, even before the appearance of a man, was enough to seize Michelle in a grip of apprehension; she got used to Kath's older boys, yet, when they engaged in some horseplay, or threw their arms around their mother, she screamed in terror, and was quite uncontrollable for some time after. Her look of fascination at being taken on a forest walk, and listening attentively to the myriads of sounds and echoes of sounds, or to seaside cliffs, where her eyes riveted onto seagulls for extraordinary long periods of time, were indicative of the severe sensory deprivation (perception) she had endured. And she continued to lie in her bed long after she had awakened, indicative perhaps of earlier experiences when even awakening was fraught with the risk of more abuse. Assessment, however, also included careful monitoring of progress, and the longer she stayed with Kath, the more obvious her progress became. Her increasing exploration of the world around her free from tension and fear, her risk taking, her ability to concentrate, the dramatic increase in appropriate emotional expressivity, all of these were confirmed as major leaps forward when she returned to the nursery after a few weeks. Kay and her colleagues at the nursery testified that this child had improved beyond recognition.

Contact and relationship between mother and child

Much time and effort was devoted to the task of 'contact'. The task alters significantly from the time that the child is initially placed with a foster parent. The first contact is usually the most problematic: the child may still be enduring some trauma as a consequence of the abuse and removal; the parent may still feel anger and hurt; the foster parent may resent contact at such an early stage. Any of these possibilities could sabotage the goal of contact. Mary was alerted to the probability that Michelle may not respond to her; she understood the reason for that. Her anger and pain were acknowledged, and she was encouraged to express it long before contact; she was able to understand that the child would sense any anger and pain, thus making contact a miserable experience for both of them. We were confident that the foster mother would be sensitive and compassionate.

The first contact took place at the nursery, where numerous toys had been made available. Michelle stood by Kath's knees for some moments. Mary was very tense, though exercised impressive self-control; she was able to restrain herself from either rushing to Michelle or beckoning her. Michelle eventually made her own way over to Mary. Mary was visibly relieved.

In the weeks that followed, contact revealed a strengthening bond between mother and child. It was characterized by mutually satisfying physical and emotional interactions. Mary became deeply committed to it; she was not easily distracted from her interest in Michelle; when she played with the child it was genuine and pleasant; she was not interested in small talk or gossip with any of the workers; she did not feel compelled to talk or play with Michelle because we were there; she didn't really mind whether we were there or not, as she obviously felt pleasure merely to be with Michelle, to have her arms around her, nursing her, in silent pride. Michelle's responses became even more demonstrative of the bond between them. She began to anticipate and look forward to seeing her mother; she became engrossed in play with her; she resisted leaving her and, eventually, she gave the foster mother a hard time each time she returned.

Comment

The principal reason for the success of contact (which gradually increased) was the attitude of the foster parent. It is highly unlikely for contact to succeed in its goals if there is a poor relationship between natural parent and foster parent. A foster mother's uncaring, critical approach to the natural mother will be sensed by both mother and child; it will induce tension in both, and it will manifest itself in the foster home to the detriment of the child. Kath's attitude to Mary was precisely the opposite; a relationship quickly developed between them which was instrumental in creating the right atmosphere for the contact, and enhanced Mary's self-confidence considerably.

Exploring mother's memories and perception of the abuse

My colleague made much progress in establishing a relationship of trust with Mary, and exploring the abuses she suffered throughout her childhood and teens, her pregnancy with Michelle, and her choice of partners. But in the main they concentrated upon her level of awareness of the abuse unintentionally perpetrated against her child. There was no difficulty in her acknowledging that Michelle had been abused; it took longer for her to identify the various types of abuse and their consequences. Many of the painful and alarming scenes involving Michelle during her periods at Chris's home, the nursery and Mary's numerous accommodations were recalled and explored in detail; Mary easily imagined what it must have been like for Michelle in any of these situations. She could do this for two basic reasons: first, she was intelligent and sensitive enough to make the imaginative leap and, secondly, and possibly more significant, Michelle's experiences were not entirely dissimilar from her own childhood experiences. The words 'emotional' and 'psychological' were no great mystery for Mary; she easily understood the difference between appropriate and inappropriate emotional responses, and how tension and conflict between carers will create a very heavy mental burden for their children. Her own past was characterized by emotional and psychological abuse, not the least damaging of which stemmed from the sexual abuse at the hands of her stepfather and the violence he perpetrated against her mother. Much attention was given to this latter type of abuse generally, and her views and feelings on the impact on Michelle in particular. Mary, too, could recall horrific moments of witnessing her mother being battered and the impact it had upon her; she remembered one particular moment, late on a Friday evening, standing shivering and trembling in her nightdress, watching helplessly, and then could stand it no longer; she dashed into the street and screamed uncontrollably until the neighbours and police came.

Towards rehabilitation

From this exploration of the past, her own as much as her child's, Mary was then invited to explore Michelle's present situation. This task was aided by video-recordings taken in the nursery and foster home (the mother's viewing was only made possible by her relationship with the foster mother; it would have been neither intelligent nor sensitive to show a mother a film of the child who had been taken off her doing wonderfully well with a foster mother who despised her!). Mary was encouraged to make comment on any part of the film, and tactfully asked to comment on specific and significant parts. She learnt to identify all the positive emotions the child was expressing and pleasantly experiencing; she appreciated the child's insatiable curiosity and constant demands for it to be satisfied; she saw Michelle engrossed in activity without fear, asserting herself both in language and in behaviour, and just simply smiling and laughing with those around her. Again it should be stressed that all these components of strategy were implemented over many months. There was no shortage of trials and tribulations. Mary wanted to throw in the towel many times. She was not the only one to have doubts; a few of the many professionals from other agencies who were also involved in the case had doubts about Mary's long-term caring capacities. These were expressed openly and honestly during countless meetings, reviews, letters and telephone conversations. My colleague persisted with Mary; so too did Mary persist with herself, increasingly coming to terms with the enormity of the abuse of Michelle, and gradually convincing us that our strategy was right.

Michelle returned to Mary. At the time of writing, they have been together eighteen months. There have been two reviews. Michelle's progress slowed slightly from the time of the return (inevitable when returning a child from an excellent foster parent to a less fortunate natural parent. This often raises alarm bells and the unspoken 'I told you so' among agencies not so directly involved; these views are predictable and the reservations behind them should be respected). My colleague and I remain convinced that the child is well placed with her mother.

Summary and conclusions

In this chapter, an attempt has been made to recreate an actual case of emotional and psychological abuse, and to record the experiences of those given the task of coping with it. The primacy of observation in such abuse cases was upheld in the value of the detailed referral about Michelle made by the nursery teacher. The social worker then had the responsibility of making similarly detailed observations in the child's home. The emotional and psychological abuse, and its grave consequences, became so obvious in Michelle's case that the workers considered protective action. They actually witnessed the terror and pain inflicted on the child, seeing her mother being subjected to one of the regular batterings she received.

Emotional and psychological abuse cases require comprehensive strategies, excellent resources, and permanency and commitment on the part of front-line workers from numerous agencies. Not the least of commitments is to the principle of facilitating as much contact as is practicably possible between mother and child. Michelle's case clearly demonstrates the importance of that principle. The triple assessment tasks of (1) facilitating and increasing contact, (2) exploring in depth the relationship between mother and child and (3) exploring the mother's perception and understanding of the type of abuse perpetrated and its consequences, all take place over a relatively long period of time; it is a necessarily continuous and cumulative process of assessment. Michelle's foster mother made a major contribution to the additional continuous assessment of the child, in particular pinpointing hitherto concealed debilitating social and behavioural consequences of the abuse. The placement was instrumental in many aspects of progress in the case.

9

IMPLICATIONS FOR MANAGEMENT AND TRAINING

Introduction

Much of what has been written in previous chapters has implications for child care management and training. This chapter will explore some of these implications. It has already been said that emotional and psychological abuse are now very much on the 'agenda' of child care workers, trainers, practitioners and magistrates. That does not imply that such agenda items will always be given due attention, nor that entrenched attitudes which always give greater priority to physical and sexual abuse will not prevail. Key personnel in the relevant agencies need to be targeted. They have to be convinced that there is a fundamental need for a rethink on the welfare concept, that is, to fully understand and accept the importance of the emotional and psychological life of the child within the overall context of the total welfare of the child. Managers and trainers cannot prepare front-line staff for tackling emotional and psychological abuse unless they ensure that staff are fully cognizant of emotional and psychological development. Nor can the latter be promoted successfully without policy, procedures and resources. Apart from the moral and professional responsibilities this implies, the Children Act makes it a legal requirement. This chapter will make recommendations which may help achieve these objectives.

A reminder of the difficulties

Some time ago, before the implementation of the Children Act 1989, I appeared before a panel, comprised of senior managers, paediatricians and health personnel, adoption specialists, legal personnel and local councillors. We were considering approval of parents for the adoption of a child for whom I had been responsible. I provided a matching report which commented in detail on the emotional, psychological and social life of the child, detailing the dramatic improvements made in all these aspects of her development. The medical personnel, however, were rightly preoccupied by another consideration: the parents smoked and the child had an asthmatic condition. These are not easy times for smokers, and we are fast approaching the day when regulations for adoption will stipulate that non-smokers only need apply (no doubt expedited by some future adopted Californian being awarded a billion dollars because the authorities allowed smoking parents to adopt him!). The interesting point about the above case is that the smoking issue didn't only dominate the discussion, but it guaranteed the exclusion of every other aspect of the child's welfare. The fact that the child had endured a shockingly high degree of emotional and psychological abuse from which social workers rescued her, and then experienced the care and commitment of the foster parents over three years, undoing all the emotional and psychological damage that had been done, and ensuring thereafter a healthy progression in her emotional and psychological life, was a matter which affected the panel not one iota. In my report, I said that the child *expressed the full range of emotions appropriately*, in marked contrast to a child who would barely express any emotion when she first arrived. I said that the parents had provided an environment *intellectually and perceptually stimulating*; that the child's *curiosity was ceaseless*, and seldom ignored; that the atmosphere in the home was sufficiently stable and tension-free to allow *her faculties of attentiveness and concentration to improve continuously*. I also spoke of the positive social and educational consequences of this progress, and said that the parents had ensured the total integration of the child within the family, extended family, school and neighbourhood. Yet not a single question or comment was made about these matters. The discussion degenerated into an argument between those who felt strongly about smoking and those who did not. The imagery of cancer and early death was invoked by the former; the latter felt compelled to acknowledge repeatedly that smoking was a terrible thing (leading to insufferable agitation oh the part of some smokers on the panel!). As the child had lived happily with the parents for most of her life, however, a majority approved of adoption.

The extent of the challenge ahead

My purpose in recalling this story is to remind readers of the core problem: yes, emotional and psychological development/abuse are on the agenda, but nothing can wipe it off so fast as concerns about physical development/abuse. This we have seen many times in preceding case material. What precisely, then, are the implications for management and trainers?

Inadequate or non-existent definition

It will be difficult to take emotional and psychological abuse seriously if the agency for which one works does not have adequate definitions for these terms. Calem and Franchi's (1989) sentiment that 'the task [of definition] is too difficult' emphasizes how little social work training has advanced on the matter. An adequate definition of emotional and psychological abuse is crucial. Readers will have had the opportunity to consider the definitions which evolved in this text. They evolved from the study of scores of definitions used by writers, agencies and government departments in Britain and elsewhere. It's not important what one thinks about these or other definitions, but it's crucially important that child care students and practitioners, particularly those with responsibility for child protection, have definitions which they can respect and apply in everyday practice.

Management's lack of training and awareness

Whatever the limitations of front-line staff in recognizing, understanding and coping with concepts like the emotional and psychological life of the child, and the reality of emotional and psychological abuse, such limitations merely reflect deficiencies in training and supervision, and the narrow focus of thought and action by those more senior personnel within their organizations. If there is a problem for newly qualified workers, then those responsible for managing and supervising them may have a much greater problem. They may have been appointed more for their managerial skills rather than their child care experience; or they have been trained and gained experience in earlier times when emotional and psychological abuse were nowhere near either the legal or training agendas. These managers are now running child care organizations. The child protection structures which they have created, and the bureaucratic and administrative machinery which serves those structures, reflect their lack of awareness and sensitivity about the emotional and psychological life of children.

As we have seen in the adoption case above, the case of Michelle in the previous chapter and the case conference mentioned in Chapter 2, managers' lack of awareness about the emotional and psychological life of children will be more obvious in their reactions to evidence or even suspicion of any kind of physical or sexual abuse. Given this reality, therefore, it would be unrealistic to expect existing management suddenly to be able to prepare and equip front-line staff for coping with the challenges of emotional and psychological abuse, i.e. identifying it, rigorously monitoring it, and jointly formulating strategies to cope with it. But a major contribution could, nevertheless, be made through changes in the administrative and bureaucratic machinery, upon which, to some extent, child protection work depends. There is little in this machinery that encourages workers to think in terms of 'emotional' and 'psychological' abuse. For example, either or both of these terms are conspicuously lacking in the forms used by most authorities for referral taking, reviews, social inquiry and case conference reports. We have also seen in earlier chapters that child protection managers avoid categorizing children on the child protection registers as being emotionally or psychologically abused even though many at the conference *feel* that's precisely what's happening to the child. Modifying the administrative and bureaucratic machinery of child protection work would concentrate the mind in respect of the task of accurately recording what is happening to the child; on the broader issue, management desperately needs self-awareness on the specific problem of why it is so vulnerable (and so reactive) to cases of physical and sexual abuse and so lethargic in response to emotional and psychological abuse. I have suggested reasons for this in Chapter 2, but answers are likely to be acted upon only if they are in response to questions posed by management itself.

On the specific machinery that we call 'child protection case conferences', these can in fact be excellent vehicles for communicating the changes recommended above, e.g. reminding conference participants that, henceforth, they will be asked about the emotional and psychological life of the child, and what precisely has been observed to indicate progressive development or impairment in either. The emotional and psychological life of the child should be a fixed item on every conference agenda. One final point on the bureaucratic machinery of child protection: recent legislative developments now permit carers to look at case files, at what has been said and written about them; even more pertinent, parents are being increasingly invited to attend case conferences. There is the risk of these developments discouraging managers from being absolutely honest with carers, particularly if it is believed that the latter are emotionally or psychologically abusing their children. Such a tendency would compromise and exacerbate the task of the front-line worker. This text has repeatedly emphasized a faith in carers' potential for knowing precisely what they have been doing to their children, wittingly or unwittingly; that potential will not be realized by administrative and bureaucratic machinery which facilitates managers avoiding the issue.

Inadequacy of existing training courses

Professional training courses for front-line child care staff such as paediatricians, social workers, health visitors, midwives, teachers and educational welfare officers, have not prepared and equipped them for defining and recognizing emotional and psychological abuse, nor for serving the victims, nor for working with the carers. None of these groups of workers emerges from their courses confident in dealing with emotional and psychological abuse, but, inevitably, paediatricians (through no choice of their own) become the recognized experts upon whom other professionals rely to articulate on the matter. In fact, paediatricians have no tested training on emotional and psychological abuse, nor do health visitors, GPs or midwives (Underwager and Wakefield, 1989). There's no reason to believe that these existing professional training courses are significantly changing to accommodate learning about emotional and psychological abuse.

This is a problem to be shared jointly by child care agencies and training establishments. They should create an adequate structure for the study of emotional and psychological abuse. Existing frameworks for the study of child protection generally should suffice, with modification and expansion, but they should also provide acceptable definition and familiarity with theories which attempt a more rigorous explanation of emotional and psychological development. Child care staff should be trained to detect emotional and psychological abuse: trainers should familiarize them with the family or societal origins of such abuse, and equip them to be able to explore those origins, and work with the victims, the family and neighbourhood protagonists central to the abuse. These have to be the basic minimum requirements for newly qualified child care workers, whether they be nursery or residential staff, health/social worker, or paediatrician.

The impact of race, gender, class and culture

Managers and trainers are acutely aware of the importance of issues like racism and gender oppression, and also the effects of poverty, class and cultural divides upon health and development generally. But we have seen in some of our case histories, that such issues have major implications for emotional and psychological development in particular. Racism is a blatant form of emotional and psychological abuse (see the case of June in Chapter 5); gender oppression, usually directed against the poorest, most deprived, inarticulate and uneducated young mothers, and often unwittingly perpetrated by child care and DSS agents as much as by brutal uncaring cohabitants (see the case of Jodie in Chapter 5), is certain to minimize the emotional and psychological care such mothers can afford to give their children. Grinding pervasive poverty can have precisely the same effect. There are major responsibilities here for managers and trainers. Enabling staff to identify the emotional and psychological impact of these conditions is a necessary first step; it could add weight to the attempts to heighten awareness and influence policy in respect of each of them.

Changing political realities

Managers and trainers cannot fail to notice the changing political context of child protection work. Until 1988, highly publicized deaths of children for whom local authorities were responsible made social work and health managers hypersensitive to the scrutiny of their political masters, and led to periodic drastic organizational changes, the appointment of additional child protection staff, and new demands on training establishments. In each of these tragedies – for example, Beckford (1985), Henry (1986), Carlile (1987) – it is obvious that the child was emotionally and psychologically abused over very long periods of time before being killed. There was seldom any mention of such abuse in the official inquiry reports and in mass media comment. Since 1988, there have been tragedies of a different kind, causing a different reaction on the part of politicians and policy makers; the recognition of child sexual abuse on a massive scale prompted over-zealous attempts by managers and their front-line staff to protect children and, in a number of cases, these efforts led to disastrous results. More generally, public inquiry reports (Hughes *et al.*, 1986; Butler-Schloss, 1988; Levy and Kahan, 1991) and court rulings (Brown, 1991) have criticized professionals' behaviour, which was inescapably emotionally and psychologically abusive. The point being made here is that public and political consciousness of emotional and psychological abuse has been heightened considerably in recent years; hundreds of children have been brought to the attention of the public and politicians not because they have been physically abused, but because they have been emotionally and psychologically abused by professional child protection workers and residential carers. This increased public consciousness should be welcome, and management and trainers in all child care agencies need to respond by increasing their own knowledge and understanding of such abuse.

The changing legal context: The Children Act

Previous child protection legislation seldom addressed the problem of emotional and psychological abuse. In contrast, the Children Act spells this out in detail: it is the authorities' duty to protect children from emotional and psychological abuse, and to promote children's emotional and psychological health (ss. 1(3), 31(9)). A more significant difference is the political climate and degree of public consciousness in which the Act and its predecessors were formulated. Preceding 1988, the public was never too interested in child care/protection legislation; in contrast, the Children Act has been steered through Parliament in an unprecedented glare of publicity and scrutiny. Management has responded vigorously to the challenges posed by the Children Act. There has been much expenditure for training programmes in social services departments. The training is welcome, but it does not lay enough emphasis upon the importance the Act attaches to emotional and psychological development. Related to this is the heavy (and gloomy) concentration on what some trainers perceive as the enormous difficulty front-line workers will now have in removing children whom they believe to be at risk. Such a perception of the Act is somewhat distorted. Yes, it will promote policies and practices formulated around the central goal of keeping children and families together, and it will ensure that child protection workers who are recommending the removal of a child know precisely what they are doing, and what they have to offer the child as an alternative. But that is not to say that the Act will make it difficult to rescue, for example, Michelle from the fear, terror and pain she endured in watching her mother being battered, or Tony from the humiliations and degradations daily inflicted upon him by his alcoholic parent. If workers from different agencies are convinced that such children are emotionally and psychologically abused, and their conviction is based upon systematic observation, developmental reports and liaison, then magistrates will be much less sceptical or hostile than those, who have been training and preparing for the Act, have been led to believe. It is unhelpful to label the Act as legislation that is going to 'make things difficult for workers'; it is more reasonable to see it as legislation concerned with the child's welfare in its widest sense, and with the longer-term strategies of those who seek to intervene on behalf of the child.

Training: The psychology base

Social work training establishments have traditionally emphasized the importance of psychology in those applying for courses. It is still widely regarded as a most relevant degree, though there appears to be a slight shift in emphasis in recent years. The Bibliography to this text will testify to the predominance of psychology in the study and research on emotional and psychological development. The traditional emphasis on psychology as 'a most relevant subject/degree' for social work training is, therefore, fully justified. A reasonable understanding of development and impairment of development will be greatly facilitated by a sound grasp of elementary developmental and abnormal psychology. Throughout this text, I have indicated that professional child care staff do not easily contemplate such aspects of development as, for example, emotion, cognition, memory, attention, perception, etc.; even less do they contemplate the causes of malfunctioning in any of these. There is a widely held feeling that such matters lie within the domain of paediatrics or psychiatry; the reality is that they lie as much within the domain of classroom teachers, educational psychologists, residential and field social workers.

Resources: An ethical as much as a priorities dilemma

Each of the many cases which have been explored throughout this text necessitate resources in rescuing or alleviating victims from the worst effects of emotional and psychological abuse. It is impossible even to contemplate the infinite number and types of resources required in coping effectively with all categories of abused children. The resources required for responding to Beverly, for example (the fifteen-year-old child psychologically abused by her newly converted fundamentalist parents), are quite different from those required to deal effectively with Tony, the child of an alcoholic parent; the latter case has an important neighbourhood dimension, necessitating distinct community work skills. There is equal variety in the resources necessary for enabling parents and carers to stop abusing their children, to enhance their own contribution to the children's progressive development. Nevertheless, resources are always an issue of priorities, and some are more glaringly obvious (or lacking) than others.

The experience, personal interest, knowledge, skill and determination which some workers have in respect of this long neglected area of child abuse, is the most valuable resource. Such workers are not likely to be gobstruck by the question, can you comment on the emotional and psychological life of the child? They will have had many years' experience of recording their regular, frequent and systematic observations of the interactions between the child and carer. They will have good liaison with key agencies, and confidence and compassion in approaching, engaging and working with the perpetrators of the abuse. They will be able to communicate and relate to particular abused children, and know at the outset their limitations in doing the same with others. Thus they will automatically enlist whatever colleague or specialist can do it better; such workers will be able to mobilize additional resources within their own and other agencies, within the community, within extended family and neighbourhood networks and, most important of all, within the parents/carers themselves. This point about the willingness to share and work with others is crucial. It is unlikely that any particular worker will have all the knowledge, experience and skill to deal with every aspect of a particular case; the origins and sustenance of emotional/psychological abuse are far too complicated for that, and the multifaceted dimensions of such cases too great for any one worker to manage effectively. As in child abuse generally, joint working is appropriate, with careful consideration given to matching the identified tasks with particular attributes of the workers from one or more agencies. This necessitates an established multidisciplinary network of observation and assessment across the key agencies, most important of which remains the school setting and the classroom teacher's unique vantage point for observing a child over a long period of time (this unobtrusive systematic observation is more preferable to the often inhibitive, clinical or office one-to-one question-and-answer setting). In many categories of such abuse, e.g. failure-to-thrive, children of mentally ill or alcoholic carers, etc., a lack of multidisciplinary cooperation – more specifically the absence of key personnel such as a health visitor or community psychiatric nurse – ensures a less than adequate service.

Managers should be particularly sensitive to workers who have no inclination, for personal, historical or other reasons, to get involved in cases of emotional and psychological abuse, e.g. babies, adolescent boys, sexually abused children – any of these may present insurmountable challenges to individual workers for numerous reasons. The reasons have to be explored, and managers have to decide whether or not the worker, through adequate counselling, support and experience, can overcome the difficulty. Nothing could be better calculated to ensure the worst possible service than ignoring these problems, and imposing such workers upon emotionally and psychologically abused children. The point is especially valid in the case of psychological damage as a consequence of sexual abuse.

There will be occasions when children as damaged emotionally and psychologically as Michelle was, will need to be removed from the unchanging climate of brutality, insecurity and impermanency responsible for the abuse. In the absence of an adequate alternative within the extended family (not an unusual realization), the local authority will have to provide. Herein is the need for the most precious resource: experienced, trained and continuously supported foster parents and residential staff who know precisely the nature of the abuse, and who have the patience, skill and commitment necessary to undo the damage caused. The foster parent's attitude to the child's parent(s) can be a crucially important factor in determining the success of the placement and the prospect of rehabilitation. Many foster parents will have nothing to do with natural parents, will refuse even to meet them; that is understandable, but unacceptable if one is seriously (as they must be) assessing and planning for rehabilitation. Regrettably, management shows no signs of acknowledging how critical the dearth of high-quality fostering and residential resources really are; in which case the Children Act, and specifically those sections which demand to know precisely what is going to happen to a child removed, will deter front-line workers from making an application to remove in the first instance. There is a more compelling and honourable reason not to remove other than the fear of being made a fool of in court: it is simply unethical to remove a child from an abusing situation without being absolutely certain about the quality of the alternative which is available. Resources are very much an ethical issue.

Research

Presumably, one of the reasons why so little has been written about emotional and psychological abuse (apart from the difficulties in defining it) is lack of research. There have been countless research projects on all aspects of psychological *development* and limited research on emotional *development*, but there is virtually no research at all on emotional and psychological *abuse*. This text has made a start in three areas; namely, exploring the impact of the abuse on emotional and psychological development, identifying behaviour which causes it, and identifying categories of parental circumstances conducive to it. The absence of research has compelled me to depend upon other types of relevant literature, my own practice experiences, and the cooperation and experiences of colleagues over twenty years. I have had access to the files of over fifty social workers over a five-year period. It is precisely those experiences which led to the identity, for example, of mentally ill, alcoholic and newly converted religious fundamentalist parents as particularly prone to unwittingly abusing their children emotionally and psychologically. It is long overdue now for professional researchers to engage in rigorous pure and applied research in these areas. The outcome may indeed contest the groups I've identified and many of the assumptions and convictions throughout this text. I'm sure that researchers will identify other situations, groups, institutions, particularly residential homes, and individual groups of carers within each of these, who may, under certain circumstances, be equally prone to emotionally and psychologically abusing.

The specific type of abuse and the reason why such carers are more likely to abuse are, of course, the key questions. Various aspects of virtually every case discussed in this text represent uncharted waters for research. There are some limitations of a practical and/or ethical nature; for example, one cannot (nor would one have any inclination to) replicate the abuse on a living child for the benefit of research (though such ethical niceties have often been absent from earlier research on deprivation; and

film and television drama appear to have little compunction about
inflicting distress on children for the benefit of a good shot), but the
research potential and its contribution to practitioners could be enormous. Many specific questions arise from previous chapters: are there
clearly differentiated impacts of the abuse on different categories of
children, children who differ in age, sex, class, culture, language,
religion, etc.? Do any of these different characteristics make a child more
vulnerable to being abused? What are the most dangerous pairing factors,
i.e. the pairing of the characteristics above with whatever characteristics
in the carers would make children especially vulnerable? Are social and
environmental factors of families, such as isolation, poverty, fragmentation, overcrowding, etc., as conducive to the abuse as most professionals (including myself) believe them to be? Are children from ethnic
minorities any more vulnerable? If so, why? What are the long-term
emotional and psychological consequences of different types of abuse on
different categories of children? How do agencies respond to such abuse
and what is the effectiveness or otherwise of that response?

There is an equally important research task for front-line workers and
managers; even more quickly and accurately than professional researchers, they can recognize changing patterns in the amounts and
types of referrals on emotional and psychological abuse. It may well be
that in their own geographical locations, there are high concentrations of
emotionally and psychologically abused children; they may be cared for
predominantly by an as yet unrecognized category of parent/carer, who
collectively and consistently abuse in a certain way; they may live in a
specific type of social and environmental milieu, and have patterns of
lifestyle and behaviour conductive to abuse. Here, indeed, for the
front-line worker and the agency they represent, would lie limitless
potential for systematic observation, knowledge, understanding and,
ultimately, for providing the abused child and carers with an effective
service. Research is much too important to be left entirely in the hands of
researchers.

General conclusion

In a case conference which I was chairing recently, my question about the
emotional and psychological life of the child to the senior personnel
representing the various agencies produced similar difficulties as those
described in previous chapters. In the same week, I was approached by a
social worker who had attended some training seminars which I gave on
emotional and psychological abuse. She said she had witnessed such
abuse during numerous supervised access visits between a five-year-old
boy and his father who had admitted sexual offences against other

children. She described how the father repeatedly and angrily prevented the child from drawing, modelling, conversing or playing with any of the standard toys and equipment specifically supplied for that purpose. The more the child persisted, the angrier the father became. The child invariably submitted, and retired to the knees of his mother, cowed and tense. The reason, of course, was father's determination to prevent any utterance or action on the child's part which could have been construed indicative of sexual abuse.

It was encouraging to learn that a recently qualified front-line colleague had observed the detail of interaction between a child and his father sufficiently enough to convince her that such interactions constituted emotional and psychological abuse: the 'sustained, repetitive inappropriate emotional responses . . . ' which 'inhibit legitimate and natural emotional expression', and the 'sustained, repetitive, inappropriate behaviour' which 'reduces the creative and developmental potential of crucially important mental faculties and processes . . . ' and will eventually 'undermine the child's attempt to understand the world around her . . . confuse and/or frighten the child, and lead to a pervasive lack of confidence'. This seems to be what the worker was describing to me.

The debate about the linkage or dichotomy between emotional and psychological development and/or abuse is a perpetual one, and readers can choose whichever stance makes more sense to them. In wearing my academic hat, I find the debate interesting, and worthy of more study and research; but, as a practitioner, I believe it has actually bred sloppiness and confusion of thought, and discouraged trainers as much as practitioners from seeking the definitions which would enable them to articulate on either aspect with confidence. Apart from the professional responsibility implied here, child care workers now face the daunting prospect of articulating in court the meaning of 'significant harm' to any or all aspects of development. The Children Act could very quickly convert the fiction of the first chapter into painful fact for some hapless workers and managers, whose reports may betray at best a lack of clarity, at worst confusion.

There are other factors which have rendered child care workers ill-prepared in articulating and coping with emotional and psychological abuse. First, their job is more complex and demanding than at any period since the Seebohm reorganizations in 1970. Secondly, the political and media scrutiny of child protection services has increased to the extent of inducing no small degree of paranoia, and discouraging managers and their front-line staff from taking an interest in anything other than physical and sexual abuse. Thirdly, the amount of unfilled vacancies remain depressingly high, increasing the pressures and sewing the seeds of disillusionment and low morale on those who stay. And, finally, child care agencies – both voluntary and statutory – seem unable to avoid plunging all too frequently into total reorganizations, leading to chronic impermanency, unreliability and unfamiliarity. All of these factors contribute not one iota towards enabling front-line staff to attain some stability, security and attitude of mind necessary for learning and preparing to cope with the problems of emotional and psychological abuse, which, by definition, are always *serious long-term problems*. Additionally, they deprive workers of reliable, adequate supervision, under which comprehensive assessments of the emotional and psychological life of the child should be made. It is ironic that as the public and mass media is becoming more critically conscious of these concepts of development and abuse, the agencies with primary responsibility for child care are repeatedly rendering themselves so chaotic and disruptive as not to be able to cope with them. Hopefully, this is only a temporary phenomenon, and heads of departments can temper their enthusiasm for reorganization with the realization of its dangers (clearly seen in inquiry reports, e.g. DHSS, 1974; Levy and Kahan, 1991).

There is, however, a factor which must ensure that managers, trainers and front-line workers alike, enhance both their understanding of the emotional and psychological life of the child, and the quality of their services to emotionally and psychologically abused children. It is the recent revelations in Britain and abroad that emotional and psychological abuse has been perpetrated by many child care professionals seeking to protect children. Surely, even a limited understanding of emotional and psychological development and an intelligent definition of emotional and psychological abuse would have discouraged senior personnel from approving the damaging interventions which took place. There are instances of severe emotional and psychological abuse which may necessitate the removal of children, but this text is as much about assessing *emotional and psychological development* in the hope and expectation that children best remain where they are; indeed, the definitions of *abuse* evolved from the literature on *development*. We now know that it was the lack of any developmental assessments which contributed to managers, social workers and police officers unwittingly inflicting emotional and psychological abuse that was, for some children, non-existent in the first instance! And, in the case of pindown and Kincora (Hughes *et al.*, 1986; Levy and Kahan, 1991), to inflict such abuse on children, many of whom were taken into care for protection from such abuse! It was a cruel irony. It is also a salutary lesson emphasizing the need to consider the *welfare of the child in its entirety* throughout all phases of child protection and child care work.

BIBLIOGRAPHY

Abramson, L. (1991) Facial expression in failure to thrive and normal infants: Implications for their capacity to engage the world. *Merrill-Palmer Quarterly*, 37(1), 159–82.

Adcock, M., White, R. and Hollows, A. (1991) *Significant Harm*. Croydon, Significant Publications.

Aldgate, J. (1991) Attachment theory and its application to child care social work: An introduction. In J. Lishman (ed.), *Handbook of Theory for Practice Teachers in Social Work*. London, Jessica Kingsley.

Allen, R. E. and Oliver, J. M. (1982) The effect of child maltreatment on language development. *Child Abuse and Neglect*, 6, 299–355.

Ammerman, R. T., Van Hasselt, V. B., Hersen, M., McGonicle, J. J. and Lubetsky, M. K. (1989) Abuse and neglect in psychiatrically hospitalized multihandicapped children. *Child Abuse and Neglect*, 13(3), 335–43.

Batchelor, J. and Kerslake, A. (1990) *Failure to Find Failure to Thrive*. London, Whiting and Birch.

Beardslee, W., Keller, M. and Klerman, G. (1985) Children of parents with affective disorder. *International Journal of Family Psychiatry*, 6, 283–99.

Benedict, M. C., White, R. B., Wulff, L. M. and Hall, B. J. (1990) Reported maltreatment in children with multiple disabilities. *Child Abuse and Neglect*, 14, 207–17.

Berwick, D. B., Levy, J. C. and Kleinerman, R. (1982) Failure to thrive: Diagnostic yield of hospitalization. *Archives of Disease in Childhood*, 57, 347–51.

Besag, V. E. (1989) *Bullies and Victims in Schools: A Guide to Understanding and Management*. Milton Keynes, Open University Press.

Bibby, P. (1991) Breaking the webb. *Social Work Today*, 3 October.

Binet, A. and Simon, T. (1905) Méthodes nouvelles pour le diagnostic du niveau intellectual des anormaux. *L'Année Psychologique*, 11, 191–244. Quoted in R. D. Gross (1987), op. cit.

Blom-Cooper, L. (1985) *A Child in Trust: Jasmine Beckford*. London, Brent.

Bott, E. (1971) Families in crisis. In J. D. Sutherland (ed.), *Towards Community Mental Health*. London, Tavistock.

Bowlby, J. (1953) *Child Care And The Growth of Love*. Harmondsworth, Penguin.

Bowlby, J. (1969) *Attachment and Loss, Vol. 1: Attachment*. London, Hogarth.

Bowlby, J. (1973) *Attachment and Loss, Vol. 2: Separation*. London: Hogarth.

Briggs, A. (1959) *The Age of Improvement*. London, Longman's Green.

Brown, E. M. (1989) *My Parent's Keeper: Adult Children of the Emotionally Disturbed*. New York, New Harbinger.

Brown, R. (1973) *A First Language – The Early Years*, London, Allen and Unwin.

Brown, Justice (1991) Judgement on Rochdale Child Sexual Abuse Investigation, 1990. Quoted in *Daily Telegraph*, 8 March, p. 3.

Budd, J. (1990) Falling short of the target. *Community Care*, 15 November, 21–2.

Butler-Sloss, E. (1988) *Report of the Enquiry into Child Abuse in Cleveland, 1987*. London, HMSO.

Calam, C. and Franchi, F. (1989) Setting basic standards. In S. Rogers, D. Hivey and E. Ash (eds), *Child Abuse and Neglect, Facing the Challenge*. Milton Keynes, Open University.

Campbell, B. (1988) *Unofficial Secrets, Child Sexual Abuse: The Cleveland Case*. London, Virago.

Camrus, A. A. (1988) Darwin revisited: An infant's first emotional facial expressions. In H. Ostler (Chair), *Emotional Expressions in Infants: New Perspectives on an Old Controversy*. Symposium conducted at the International Conference on Infant Studies, Washington D.C. Quoted in Malatesta *et al.* (1989), op. cit.

Carroll, J. and Williams, P. (1988) Talking to toddlers. *Community Care*, 31 March, pp. 20–2.

Channel 4 (1992) *Dispatches*, London, 19 February.

Choo, C. (1991) Aboriginal children 1990 and the international convention on the rights of the child. *Children Australia*, 15(2), 15–19.

Cohen, G., Eysenck, M. W. and Le Voi, M. (1986) *Memory: A Cognitive Approach*. Milton Keynes, Open University Press.

Coleman, L. (1989) Learning from the McMartin hoax. *Issues in Child Abuse Accusations, Institute of Psychological Therapies*, 1(2), 68–71.

Conte, J. R. (1982) Sexual abuse of children: Enduring issues for social workers. *Journal of Social Work and Human Sexuality*, 1/2, 1–19.

Coster, W. J., Gersten, M., Beeghly, M. and Cicchetti, D. (1989) Communicative functioning in maltreated toddlers. *Developmental Psychology*, 25(6), 1020–9.

Curtis, R. (1980) Bob: Settling into a group. In S. Murgatroyd (ed.), *Helping the Troubled Child: Interprofessional Case Studies*. London, Harper and Row.

Dale, P., Davies, M., Morrison, T. and Waters, J. (1986) *Dangerous Families*. London, Tavistock.

Darwin, C. (1872) *The Expressions of the Emotions in Man and Animals*. London, Murray.

Department of Health (1988) *Protecting Children: A Guide for Social Workers Undertaking Comprehensive Assessment*. London, HMSO.

Department of Health (1990) *Social Services Inspectorate: Inspection of Child Protection Services in Rochdale*. London, HMSO.

Department of Health (1991) *Working Together*. London, HMSO.

Department of Health and Social Security (1974) *Report of the Committee of Enquiry into the Care and Supervision Provided in Relation to Maria Colwell*. London, HMSO.

Devereux, E. C., Bromfenbrenner, U. and Suci, G. J. (1962) Patterns of parent behaviour in the USA and Federal Republic of Germany: A cross-national comparison. *International Social Sciences Journal*, 14, 488–506.

Eaton, L. (1991) Ritual abuse: Fantasy or reality. *Social Work Today*, September.

Finkelhor, D., Williams, L. M. and Burns, N. (1988) *Nursery Crimes: Sexual Abuse in Day Care*. New York, Sage.

Franklin, B. and Parton, N. (1991) *Social Work, the Media and Public Relations*. London, Routledge.

Furnell, J. R. G. (1987) Emotional abuse – the forgotten option? *Social Work Today*, 12 March.

Furniss, T. (1991) *The Multi-professional Handbook of Child Sexual Abuse*. London, Routledge.

Garbarino, J., Guttman, E. and Seeley, J. W. (1986) *The Psychologically Battered Child*. San Francisco, Jossey Bass.

Garbarino, J., Brookhouser, P. E. and Authier, K. J. (1987) *Special Children, Special Risks: The Maltreatment of Children with Disabilities*. New York, Aldine De Gruyter.

Gomes-Schartz, B., Horowitz, J. M. and Cardarelli, A. P. (1990) *Child Sexual Abuse: The Initial Effects*. New York, Sage.

Goodman, G. S., Hirschman, J. E., Hepps, D. and Rudy, L. (1991) Children's memory for stressful events. *Merrill-Palmer Quarterly*, 37(1), 109–57.

Greenwich Borough (1987) *A Child in Mind: The Protection of Children in a Responsible Society*. The Report of the Commission of Enquiry into the Death of Kimberley Carlile. London, Borough of Greenwich.

Griffiths, P. (1980) John: Rejection and perception. In S. Murgatroyd (ed.), *Helping the Troubled Child*. London, Harper and Row.

Gross, R. D. (1987) *Psychology: The Science of Mind and Behaviour*. London, Arnold.

Harbinson, J. (1989) *Growing Up in Northern Ireland*. Belfast, Stranmillis College.

Harper, J. (1989) The watcher and the watched. *Adoption and Fostering*, 13(2), 15–20.

Harper, J. (1991) What about the wounded? *Social Work Today*, 12 December.

Harris, P. L. (1989) *Children and Emotion: The Development of Psychological Understanding*. Oxford, Basil Blackwell.

Helfer, R. E. and Kempe, H. C. (eds) (1968/1980) *The Battered Child*, 1st and 3rd edns. Chicago, University of Chicago Press.

Hirschberg, L. (1990) When infants look to their parents: 12 month olds' response to conflicting parental emotional signals. *Child Development*, 61, 1187–91.

Howell, S. (1981) Rules not words. In P. Heelas and A. Lock (eds), *Indigenous Psychologies*. London, Academic Press.

Hubert, J. (1992) *Social Policy Research Findings*, No. 18. York, Joseph Rowntree Foundation.

Hughes, W. H., Patterson, W. J. and Whalley, H. J. (1986) *Report of the Committee of Enquiry into Children's Homes and Hostels*. Belfast, DHSS.

Iwaniec, D., Herbert, M. and McNeish, A. S. (1985) Social work with failure to thrive children and their families, Part 1. Psychosocial factors. *British Journal of Social Work*, 15, 243–59.

Jaffe, P. G., Wolfe, D. A. and Wilson, S. K. (1990) *Children of Battered Women.* New York, Sage.

Jones, C. and Novak, T. (1991) Soapbox. *Social Work Today*, 12 December.

Jones, D. P. H., Bentovim, A., Cameron, H., Vizard, E. and Walkind, S. (1991) Significant harm in context: the child psychiatrist's contribution. In M. Adcock *et al.* (1991), op. cit.

Jordan, W. and Packman, J. (1978) Training for social work with violent families. In J. P. Martin (ed.), *Violence in the Family*. Chichester, John Wiley.

Keller, M., Beardslee, W., Dorer, D. and Lovani, P. (1986) Impact of severity and chronicity of parental affective illness on adaptive functioning and psycho-pathology in children. *Archives of General Psychiatry*, 43, 930–57.

Kennedy, M. (1988) The abuse of deaf children. *Child Abuse and Neglect*, 13(5), 3–6.

Laking, P. (1988) Appearances can be deceptive. *Community Care*, 25 February, pp. 26–7.

Lee, K. (1991) The healing way. *Community Care*, 27 June, pp. 24–5.

Leeds Social Service Department (1987) *Tip of the Iceberg*. Leeds, Leeds Social Services.

Levy, A. and Kahan, B. (1991) The Pindown experience and the protection of children: A report of the Staffordshire Child Care Inquiry. Staffordshire, Staffordshire County Council.

Lincoln General Hospital (1988) *Family Intervention* (Information Circular). Lincoln, Nebraska.

Lourie, I. and Stefano, L. (1978) On defining emotional abuse. In *Proceedings of the Second Annual National Conference on Child Abuse and Neglect*. Washington, D.C., US Government Printing Office.

Malatesta, C. Z., Culver, C., Tesman, J. and Shepherd, B. (1989) The development of emotional expression during the first two years of life. *Monographs of the Society for Research in Child Development*, Serial No. 219.

Matthews, C. (1991) The pawns of Brindise. *Independent Magazine*, 23 March.

Melville, J. and Bean, P. (1990) *Lost Children of the Empire*. London, Unwin Hyman.

Morgan, S. R. (1987) *Abuse and Neglect of Handicapped Children*. Boston, College Hill.

Morrice, J. K. W. (1976) *Crisis Intervention in the Community*. Oxford, Pergamon.

Mrazek, P. B. and Mrazek, D. A. (1981) The effects of child sexual abuse. In P. B. Mrazek and C. H. Kempe (eds), *Sexually Abused Children and Their Families*. Oxford, Pergamon Press.

Murgatroyd, S. (ed.) (1990) *Helping the Troubled Child*. London, Harper and Row.

Newsome, J. and Newsome, E. (1963) *Patterns of Infant Care in an Urban Community*. London, Allen and Unwin (Harmondsworth, Penguin, 1972).

Newsome, J. and Newsome, E. (1974) Cultural aspects of childrearing in the English-speaking world. In M. P. M. Richards (ed.), *The Integration of a Child into a Social World*. Cambridge, Cambridge University Press.

Newsome, J. and Newsome, E. (1986) Protecting children from parental physical punishment. In *Contributions to the Children's Legal Seminar*, 21 July. London, Approach Ltd.

Oates, J. and Sheldon, S. (eds) (1987) *Cognitive Development in Infancy*. Milton Keynes, Open University.

O'Hagan, K. P. (1980) Is social work necessary? *Community Care*, 297, 24–6.

O'Hagan, K. P. (1984) Family crisis intervention in social services. *Journal of Family Therapy*, 6, 149–81.

O'Hagan, K. P. (1986) There isn't an effective crisis training program. *Social Work Today*, 29 September.

O'Hagan, K. P. (1989) *Working with Child Sexual Abuse*. Milton Keynes, Open University Press.

O'Hagan, K. P. (1991) Crisis intervention in social work. In J. Lishman (ed.), *Handbook of Theory for Practice Teachers in Social Work*. London, Jessica Kingsley Publishers.

Ortony, A., Clore, G. L. and Collins, C. (1988) *The Cognitive Structure of Emotions*. Cambridge, Cambridge University Press.

Oster, H. (1978) Facial expression and affect development. In M. Lewis and L. A. Rosenblum (eds), *The Development of Affect*. New York, Plenum.

Piaget, J. (1950) *The Psychology of Intelligence*. London, Routledge and Kegan Paul.

Pollitt, E., Eichler, A. and Chan, C. (1975) Psychosocial development and behaviour of mothers of failure-to-thrive children. *American Journal of Orthopsychiatry*, 45(4), 525–37.

Ratner, H. H. and Stettner, L. J. (1991) Thinking and feeling: Putting Humpty Dumpty together again. *Merrill-Palmer Quarterly*, 37(1), 1–24.

Ray, R. (1991) Consequences of parental illness on children: A review. *Social Work and Social Sciences Review*, 2(2).

Reiner, B. S. and Kaufman, I. (1959) *Character Disorder in Parents of Delinquents*. New York, Family Service Association of America.

Richards, M. P. M. (1974) First steps in becoming social. In M. P. M. Richards (ed.), *The Integration of a Child into a Social World*. Cambridge, Cambridge University Press.

Richardson, K. (1991) *Understanding Intelligence*. Milton Keynes, Open University Press.

Rohner, R. P. (1980) Worldwide tests of parental acceptance– rejection theory: An overview. *Behaviour Science Research*, 15, 1–21.

Roland, E. (1989) Bullying: The Scandanavian research tradition. In D. P. Tattum and D. A. Lane (eds), *Bullying in Schools*. Stoke-on-Trent, Trentham Books.

Rosaldo, M. Z. (1980) *Knowledge and Passion*. Cambridge, Cambridge University Press.

Saarni, D. (1979) Children's understanding of display rules for expressive behaviour. *Developmental Psychology*, 15, 424–9.

Schachter, S. and Singer, J. E. (1962) Cognition, social and physiological determinants of emotional states. *Psychological Review*, 69, 379–99.

Schmitt, B. D. (ed.) (1978) *The Child Protection Handbook*. New York, Garland STPM Press.

Schneider, C. J. (1982) The Michigan Screening Profile of Parenting. In R. H. Starr (ed.), *Child Abuse Prediction: Policy Implications*. Cambridge, Mass., Ballinger.

Sills, R. H. (1978) Failure to thrive. *American Journal of Diseased Children*, 132, 967–9.

Smetana, J. G. (1981) Preschool children's conceptions of moral and social rules. *Child Development*, 52, 1333–6.

Smith, S. M. (ed.) (1978) *The Maltreatment of Children*. London, MTP Press.

Smith, S. M., Hanson, R. and Noble, S. (1973) Parents of battered babies; A controlled study. *British Medical Journal*, IV, 388–91.

Spitz, R. (1945) Hospitalism: an enquiry into the genesis of psychiatric conditions in early childhood. *Psychoanalytic Study of the Child*, 1, 53–61.

Steele, B. F. and Pollock, C. B. (1968) A psychiatric study of parents who abuse infants and small children. In R. E. Helper and C. H. Kempe (eds), *The Battered Child*. Chicago, University of Chicago Press.

Tate, T. (1991) *Children for the Devil*. London, Methuen.

Tattum, D. P. and Lane, D. A. (eds) (1989) *Bullying in Schools*. Stoke-on-Trent, Trentham Books.

Tomkins, S. (1962) *Affect, Imagery and Consciousness: The Positive Affects*, Vol. 1. New York, Springer.

Tomkins, S. (1962) *Affect, Imagery and Consciousness: The Negative Affects*, Vol. 2. New York, Springer.

Underwager, R. and Wakefield, H. (1989) *Investigation and Trial Preparation in Cases of Child Sexual Abuse*. Springfield, Ill., Thomas.

Van Leishout, C. F. M. (1975) Young children's reactions to barriers placed by their mothers. *Child Development*, 46, 879–86.

Vernon, M. D. (1962) *The Psychology of Perception*. London, Pelican.

Vernon, P. E. (1979) *Intelligence: Heredity and Environment*. San Francisco, W. H. Freeman.

Verster, J. M. (1987) Human cognition and intelligence: towards an integrated theoretical perspective. In S. H. Irvine and S. E. Newstead (eds), *Intelligence and Cognition: Contemporary Frames of Reference*. Dordrecht, Martinus Nijhoff.

Walford, G. (1989) Bullying in public schools: Myth and reality. In D. P. Tattum and D. A. Lane (eds) *Bullying in Schools*. Stoke-on-Trent, Trentham Books.

Walker, L. (1984) Intervention by criminal justice agencies: spouse abuse. Paper prepared for *Working Meeting on Family Violence as a Criminal Justice Problem*. National Institute of Justice, Washington D.C., 25–7 October. Quoted in J. Garbarino *et al.* (1986), op. cit.

Watson, G. (1989) The abuse of disabled children and young persons. In W. S. Rogers, D. Hevey and E. Ash (eds) *Child Abuse and Neglect*. London, Batsford.

Watson, J. B. and Morgan, I. (1917) Emotional reactions and psychological experimentation. *American Journal of Psychology*, 28, 161–74.

Wesley, J. (1872) *Works*. London, Wesleyan Conference Office.

White, R., Carr, P. and Lowe, N. (1990) *A Guide to the Children Act 1989*. London, Butterworth.

Whiting, L. (1976) In *Proceedings of the Second Annual National Conference on Child Abuse and Neglect*, Washington, D.C., US Government Printing Office.

Widdowson, E. M. (1951) Mental contentment and physical growth. *Lancet*, 260, 1316–18.

Winnicott, W. (1971) *Playing and Reality*. Harmondsworth, Penguin.

Woititz, J. G. (1983) *Adult Children of Alcoholics*. Florida, Health Communication Inc.

Wyatt, G. E. and Powell, G. J. (1988) *The Lasting Effects of Child Sexual Abuse*. London, Sage.

INDEX